Almost Home

Setting Our Sights
Toward Heaven

ALMOST *Home*

David Steen

NASHVILLE

NEW YORK • LONDON • MELBOURNE • VANCOUVER

Almost Home

Setting Our Sights Toward Heaven

Published in New York, New York, by Morgan James Publishing. Morgan James is a trademark of Morgan James, LLC. www.MorganJamesPublishing.com

Proudly distributed by Publishers Group West®

Scripture taken from the New King James Version®. Copyright © 1982 by Thomas Nelson. Used by permission. All rights reserved.

ISBN 9781636981277 paperback
ISBN 9781636981284 ebook
Library of Congress Control Number:
2023930483

Cover & Interior Design by:
Christopher Kirk
www.GFSstudio.com

Morgan James is a proud partner of Habitat for Humanity Peninsula and Greater Williamsburg. Partners in building since 2006.

Get involved today! Visit: www.morgan-james-publishing.com/giving-back

To my Lord and Savior Jesus Christ:
Thank you for calling me to Your saving grace
and making the journey possible.

To Dad and Mom:
You have continued to bring me strength
and encouragement every step of the way.

To my sweet and lovely bride:
You are my best friend, my biggest fan, my little blue-eyed storm.
We did it, baby!

To our children:
Andrew, Coady, Zachary, Reagan, Bradley, Hannah, Holly,
Joshua, and Olivia. You have lived this journey with us
every step of the way. We are blessed by God to have you!

To our family and friends:
We are blessed beyond measure to have so many of you
who have encouraged, supported, and blessed us along this journey.
God has used so many of you to make us who we are for Him.
We will be forever grateful!

Table of Contents

viii | Almost *Home*

Introduction

The Time Has Come

If you don't have anything to say, then don't say it.
Olivia, age 5

L et that sink in a bit. At the ripe old age of five, our little Olivia put together that phrase based on something she had heard come out of our mouths many times over: "If you don't have anything nice to say, then don't say anything at all."

Well, I do in fact have something to say—several things, actually—and I've been stewing on it for many years.

Speaking of stewing, on one of my recent diet kicks, after having raised some beef on our farm and filled our freezer to the brim, I discovered the value of soup bones. Now, I've made soup and chili before and know the difference between something that has been thrown together in thirty minutes and something that has simmered for hours on end. But when I pulled out those soup bones from our farm-raised, grass-fed steer, I learned something else entirely, and the aftereffects made the dogs on the farm oh-so-sad.

You see, when you really understand the value of a good package of soup bones, you put them in the crockpot for a full day—I mean a *full* twenty-four hours—to pull all of the real nutrients out of the bones, from the inside out. Having done so a few times, I have discovered that when you cook those bones down, allowing the marrow to emerge from the inside and soak into the onions, carrots, celery, mushrooms, and other seasonings—well, it's a pot of stew like no other. Those with an appreciation come running; they've smelled it cooking in the house for a full day. There's nothing like waking up in the morning to the rich aroma of bone broth stew in your nostrils. And what about the dogs? Well, I've learned that when those bones are cooked and all the nutritional value is in what I'm eating, the dogs don't care a lick about those bones. They just walk away, wondering why I'm offering them something so vile.

A few years back, I had the privilege of spending some time with a bestselling Christian author. This author is a pastor and leader in the Church who has done and continues to do amazing things to further the Kingdom of our Lord. I remember a story he told about when he was younger, in the early part of his ministry, and how he thought he was ready to write a book. His message was on the forefront of his mind, and he was anxious to scream it the hilltops. One day, during a ministry event with a very famous elder evangelist, he shared with him his passion about writing the book. The evangelist listened to him intently, then looked at him and said something like, "You haven't been around long enough to have anything to write about. Get with me in ten years, and then we'll talk."

He was stunned at the evangelist's straightforward response, but nonetheless, he took note of it and focused his energies in other areas until he was ready to write the book God had for him to write. It took time and experience to cultivate what was needed to bring his best, to gain experiences he had not even known about a decade earlier. That proved successful for the once-young and inexperienced pastor: waiting on God to work it out in His perfect timing helped him to create exactly the book God desired. The time of waiting, or "stewing," blessed him immensely.

In the early part of our marriage, as our family was growing, I too had the desire to write a book to tell the stories of what God had been doing in our family's life. Others encouraged me to write those stories and to share about our unbelievable experiences. I recently looked back at some of those earlier writings, stories I had shared with others in a blog. I couldn't believe some of it! As I read aloud, my wife, my biggest fan, cringed, saying, "Wow, it's hard to believe you wrote that." What she meant in her own special way was, *That could sure use some polishing.* I couldn't have agreed with her more.

You Can't Make This Up

Many people wake up each day and go about their business in their crazy, busy lives, never experiencing anything out of the ordinary. My heart goes out to those poor souls. Many folks who have been around me for a short time may think *I* am stuck in my beloved routines, going about life blind to the extraordinary things going on around me. Yet I am far from it.

Don't get me wrong: I like predictable. I breathe it and eat it. Predictability oozes from my pores when I sweat. Just ask my sweet wife of over two decades, the helpmate God has blessed me with, who complements me in all the ways in which I am deficient. She will attest to my predictability and my love for it. Or ask my dear, patient children, who have had to put up with my desire for everything to be just right and perfect at all times. Yes, I like a meal on time. I like *being* on time and expect others to respect me and do the same. The consistency of the mail coming, the sun rising, great coffee, and the same bedtime—these things excite me. So, how could a guy like me, Mr. Consistent, the fellow who loves an ordinary existence, get excited about a loving God who walks into my existence anytime He wants and shakes me to the core? Well, I can tell you—it's because my God is always faithful, right on time, and never disappoints—creating a life experience like no other!

I consider myself blessed. The core of my inner being has been shaken by God more times than I can count. Many naysayers of the world, including those closest to me, have wagged their heads and chalked it up to coincidence or me not knowing what I am talking about. But in more than my fair share of times, when I'm bragging on God in a story to someone, I have said the words, "You couldn't make this stuff up if you tried!" I think God enjoys being the most prolific mystery writer of all time, putting clues around us to help us know He's watching and looking out for us when we pay attention.

Naysayers, beware. If you are one to always be the skeptic, always having something negative to say or never wanting to give God credit for working in a person's life in a way that makes no sense to you, stop reading now. You should not proceed. Your thinking will be challenged. You will say things like, "That's stupid," or, "He just made that up," or, "There's no way!" or, "That's just a coincidence."

Stop. Read no further. Pass this book on to a more worthy soul. You've been warned.

Now, for the open minded, those who want to drink in the flood of things that have happened to my family, real things we experienced that only God can do, welcome. Expect greatness not from us, but from our loving and righteous God, the one true living God. My hope is that our stories will help you know life is full of seasons, challenges, growth, and change. Those times are opportunities, not obstacles. When things seem impossible and the mountains in front of you seem immovable, remember nothing is impossible with God.

As the chorus lines of the old hymn "Blessed Assurance," ring out:

This is my story, this is my song,
Praising my Savior all the day long.

1

From Concrete to Dirt

We were suburban city kids, my sister and I. The memories of our house in Southern California do not include bugs, especially not ticks or chiggers. Concrete was an integral part of our existence, the stepping stone that took us where we were going, whether it was walking to school or down the street to visit a neighbor. We did have a yard complete with grass and trees, a small garden, and some space for our pets to roam. We were the typical American family of four.

My dad, a lifelong Navy veteran, served his country faithfully all around the globe. Dad and Mom always talked about the places we lived after my sister and I arrived on the scene and the Navy moved us around, but my memories of childhood essentially include two places: our suburban home in Southern California, with its sidewalk to skateboard on and neighbor kids to play with, and the other side of the planet we landed after that—Arkansas.

Our Southern California home was a modest house in the suburbs somewhat near where my dad was stationed in the Navy. My dad always had a knack for building things. It seemed like there was nothing he couldn't put together. If you could dream it, Dad could build it.

In those early years, Dad built my sister and me a small playhouse with a sandbox beside it which, looking back, was likely not any larger than a small lawnmower shed. But it was all my sis and I needed, somewhere for us to pretend, to dream about our own place one day, to play house. We had a nice fenced-in backyard with a few pets including rabbits, a weenie dog, and a desert tortoise named George. At times, we saw owls in the large tree in the middle of our backyard. We had some kids to play with next door and other friends down the street. That was our life. That was home.

Though we dwelled in the suburbs, our family treasured camping and fishing in those early years in California. I didn't understand why we wanted to get away for the weekend, as I enjoyed growing up in our neighborhood. But I have wonderful memories of going to campgrounds in our camper, hanging around with family and friends, fishing, and eating special things we didn't normally get at home. Camping was our little home away from home. It was a time to take our bicycles somewhere else and ride around in a new place. It meant getting close to nature before I ever knew there was a God who created it all.

On one such adventure, I made a point to explore a short distance from our campsite to see if I could stake my own claim. Somehow, that had been taught to me at an early age, to all of us,

I suppose: find yourself a place to call home, establish your castle, dig the moat, and defend it.

I found just the place, minus the moat. Not far from our campsite was an outcropping of huge boulders that had trees growing up all around them. Ducking through a narrow passage between the rocks, I discovered a solitary place, a cave of sorts right inside the rocks with a canopy of trees above. I set out to make that place my own, as if no one else on the planet had ever discovered it in that well-established park before. Boys have a way of letting their imaginations take them to places unseen, and I was no different. I crafted my little hideout for the weekend, sweeping the dirt floor and setting up house. Every moment I could, I would venture off from our campsite and go to my new abode. When the weekend ended and it was time to head back to reality, back to the city, I had to bid my little hideout farewell.

For many children, the concept of home begins with a big cardboard box from an appliance delivery that in short order becomes a fort. You cut windows, identify a door, then go and fix a peanut butter and jelly sandwich to bring back and eat in your "house." The desire for a place to call home seems to be hardwired into us by the Creator. I believe it is indeed.

What starts as a box, a fort, a campsite, or a playhouse soon becomes, in our developing imaginations, the home we wish for all our lives, our dream home. We watch our parents stake their claim and provide a home for us, and then we are determined to do it even better, to one-up them. This is not borne of malicious greed in most cases; it is something we pick up on in our early years. What our parents have acquired, what they have achieved, we want to show them we can do as well as they have done and then some.

This pursuit of home can be unhealthy for many, leading folks to their demise in a variety of ways. Many a household has seen this destruction. A job loss, business failure, or some other unforeseen event can bring life crashing down. Or worse yet, a husband, his wife, or both get caught up in the never-ending web of work success, which drives them to get a bigger house, more cars, boats, campers (to get away from the home they wanted so badly!), and a plethora of other things. This is a huge trap, competing with everyone else around, commonly referred to as "keeping up with the Joneses." All those neighbors of ours, including the Jones family, are generally as stressed out as we are about keeping up, but most of us are not brave enough to admit it.

My dad grew up in much more humble beginnings than our suburban home. Dad was the ninth and youngest child in a long line of brothers and sisters born in the first half of the twentieth century. Dad came along toward the end of the Great Depression, not long before World War II. He was born in a log cabin in North Central Arkansas, deep in the heart of hillbilly country in a place most people may never get off the beaten path to see.

Amazingly, the old family home where my grandmother (whom I never met) gave birth to Dad and many of my uncles and aunts is still standing today, along with the other family cabin on the next ridge a stone's throw away. The owner of the property has gone to great lengths to keep those old structures intact, preserving the symbols of our family heritage. It is now over a hundred years old, and we visit as often as we can to get photos and think back on the days when Dad and his siblings roamed the place, as well as their family before them. Living off the land was all there was. Most of the family escaped the so-called trappings of those country homes and primitive existence, but one lone survivor stayed to the bitter end: my dad's uncle Lesco Steen, otherwise known as Uncle Led.

The road into the wild, to the country where life began for my dad, was a winding, two-lane adventure, an adventure we pursued on vacation a few years prior to permanently moving to Arkansas. Dad had been there a lot to visit relatives and his old homeplace, but not with us and not quite like this. It was one thing to visit Arkansas, to arrive on an interstate highway in the River Valley, and quite another thing to take a two-lane, switchback-curved road for miles and miles into the wilderness. Thus began our relationship with Uncle Led, the lone remaining caretaker of the homeplace.

Arriving a few miles north of Marshall, Arkansas, we turned down what most would call a dirt trail. California-state-park-city-kid camping was over. We were entering the *real* wild! After squeezing our trailer up and down a rock-covered, one-lane road, we arrived at what seemed like a place in the world where time stood still or had maybe been forgotten.

Although many of Dad's uncles were alive and well in other parts of the area, Uncle Led was the remaining member of the family who made the original place his home, deep in the heart of Searcy County, Arkansas. He welcomed us with open arms. We stayed in our camper there for a while and came to know this old-timer who seemed like a relic to me. The visit included sitting on the old cabin porch of the original family cabin that had been built in the nineteenth century, which Uncle Led still lived in—no electricity, no running water, no plumbing, and of course, no phone. Our camper was the closest thing to a modern convenience for miles around.

Sitting on that old porch, worn down by decades of weather, rocking chairs, and stories, we enjoyed the company of our new-found great-uncle. He enjoyed us immensely as well. He told us about times of old, laughed, and played his handmade banjo as he sang to entertain us. When we were thirsty, we were introduced to a bucket that sat on a shelf on the porch, equipped with a large metal ladle to drink from. Down the hill, halfway to the other family cabin, was a covered spring. This was the source of the water in the bucket, and it provided an ample supply of fresh water.

As a young boy, tasting that precious mountain spring water from our family source, a strange wave came over me. Something about putting that tin dipper to my mouth and drinking in that luscious, untainted source of life altered something in my being. There was a certain dizziness I can't explain, a spiritual occurrence that overtook my soul. There is still something mesmerizing about that place that stirs my soul to the core. Even the journey there, with all its hills and valleys, twists and turns, invokes a passion in me that longs for home.

The water from that mountain spring is no match for the Source of my deliverance from this mortal existence, the sojourning of this temporary life. Ah, when you can drink from the well of eternal existence provided through the Lord Jesus Christ, a spiritual awakening takes place: an exuberance, a deep longing for otherworldliness that penetrates the depth of your existence.

While you may find a host of other springs in this life that consume you with the lusts of the flesh, none can compare to the living water Christ brings.

Uncle Led barely had anything, yet he seemed as happy as one could be living out there in solitude. An old cracker tin was the storage container for sticks of Doublemint gum he acquired on some of his treks to the nearest town several miles away. He was happy to share the gum with my sister and me. I remember it being somewhat firm, and there was no telling how old it was, but we didn't care and were happy to get it. It brought a twinkle to his eyes to see us enjoy his generous gift. When it was time to pack up the camper and head back down the long road toward home, Uncle Led, always the sensitive one, cried and cried as we left and begged us to come back soon. We continued to visit as often as possible once we settled down later in the Arkansas River Valley.

When I was seven, Dad bid the Navy farewell after twenty years of faithful service to our country. We packed up our things in California and prepared to move back "home," although I thought home was where we were. We were on our way to Arkansas, the land of opportunity, where Dad and Mom had their humble beginnings. We were venturing out on the longest camping trip ever, one in which we packed everything we owned, never to return. We were headed to the country, trading concrete for dirt.

My California memories of country life included a field trip during kindergarten and first grade to a local farm. Dairy cows and hay were implanted in my brain on those outings. Little did I know how much I would learn to appreciate hay—

all I ever wanted and then some—when we moved to God's country, Arkansas, where they seemingly bred ticks, chiggers, and snakes to run off city people like us. To think that Dad and Mom had *come* from this primitive place that I would later fondly refer to as home!

After arriving in Arkansas in the summer of 1976, we had nowhere to live except the camper we had spent many a camping trip in. I was soon introduced to country living, where sidewalks did not exist. Skateboards were scoffed at as unnecessary evils incapable of traversing across gravel or dirt roads. That was okay with me because my grandpa, whom I hadn't known much about until then, lived in a tiny trailer of his own near a creek. He didn't have much, but he didn't seem to care. I learned to eat beans and tomatoes that came from gardens and played by the creek any-time I wanted that summer. An amazing bonus was that I learned how to burn our trash since nobody in this part of the world had apparently heard of a garbage truck. A seven-year-old boy with matches? What an adventure!

That summer we became "Arkies." Dad and Mom were already Arkies, but I never knew it until our move as we accli-mated to the humidity, working outside a lot, and seeing all manner of critters including ticks, chiggers, and snakes. Snakes were cool, though, because seeing one meant we would see my one-and-a-half armed grandpa wield a .410 shotgun to bring those crawling varmints to their early demise, along with what-ever else was nearby when the dust settled.

Grandpa, Mom's dad, amazed me. Although he had quite a humble place to live in his small trailer, he didn't seem to need anything aside from powdered Garrett snuff and Dr. Pepper. He was born with only half of his left arm, which extended just past his elbow. At the end of his "nub," right where he bent his elbow, were little "dots," which were likely his fingers that had never formed. The word "handicapped" hadn't been invented in those days. He was always happy to demonstrate his strength on me as he held me in a headlock with his half arm while I wriggled and screamed. Grandpa did what he had to do to take care of himself and his family, and I remember my mom and her two brothers fondly referring to him as "Daddy."

Aside from my adventures on the creek that summer, I saw a tractor driven for the first time ever, by my grandpa of course. This was his home and he was established. Across the way, just a short distance down the road, lived my mom's first cousin and his family, who were fondly attached to my grandpa, whom they called Uncle Homer. Grandpa was quite the farmhand for them, helping in all that needed doing from mowing and baling hay to growing a garden. Hard work was a necessary function of life that I am glad to have inherited.

The land where we settled was on ten acres just down the road from Grandpa's place. He had selected the land for us long before Dad left the Navy and negotiated its purchase from another local farmer, Mr. Pigg (yes, that really was his name!), who would soon become our neighbor. The Arkansas River Valley in west-central Arkansas became my home for the remainder of my growing up years and beyond. While it was a considerable distance south from where Dad had been born in the cabin, that centrally located place was ideal for Dad to find work. It was near Mom's family and within reasonable driving distance of several relatives in multiple directions, whose homes we began to frequent as time permitted.

Living within driving distance of Dad's family as well as Mom's, we began to meet many relatives I never even knew we had.

Not long into our adventure as Arkansas residents, we settled into a single-wide mobile home on our property, and Dad and Mom started to work on a new house. California became a distant memory, a place in the past. Concrete sidewalks were replaced by gravel roads, and we were in our own little piece of heaven. We were home.

Living in the Arkansas River Valley afforded us many opportunities to enjoy the outdoors. We especially loved frequenting a large, nearby lake to swim in during the summer. On many of those trips, we would pass fancy houses along that lakefront drive, and one that seemed quite desirable kept grabbing my attention. On one of our trips to the lake past that house, I told my mom, "Someday, when I get rich, I'm going to buy you a house like that to live in." Now why would a young boy say that to his mother? Dad had done an amazing job of providing us a nice place to live and everything we needed, but for some reason, that desire to conquer welled out of me like an overflowing spring of water. I suppose it was linked to a man's desire to find a wife and provide her a home, but the only woman for me at that time was Mom, thank the good Lord! There I was, making proclamations about things I knew little about. Boys will be boys!

Thus continued the longing in my young heart: the desire to stake my claim, to have my own place to call home. What started in a playhouse in the backyard and a hideout at a campground became my dream of having a place to call my own. Watching and experiencing firsthand as my dad and mom developed their dream and visited the old family cabins in the wild firmly embedded in me that desire. My sights were set. I would get an education, get a good job, and find my dream home one day.

Certainly, that thought process was drilled into our heads by our parents, school, and society at large: get an education, get a good job, get married, start a family, move into your dream house, work at your job for decades, and retire in a porch swing sitting by your sweetheart. That was the plan.

Another house I recall passing several times in my early years also impressed me. It wasn't such a big house, but the cool thing about it was that it had three stories. Wow! Wouldn't that be cool? I never knew a single soul who had a house with three levels in it. That idea took root and lay dormant for years, slowly growing in the back of my mind.

Life has a way of getting away from you like a runaway freight train, or at least getting you sidetracked, taking you down roads you never intended to turn down. Yes, I grew up, completed my education, and took the lifelong job I'd always hoped for. The seeds of desire for home had been scattered on the fertile soil of my existence, watered by springs of pure water from the experiences of my family upbringing. Although the seeds were germinating and ready to burst into the growth of my future, home would have to wait, at least for a time.

One thing I should have paid close attention to was that my grandpa and my great uncle both seemed to be marvelously satisfied with their simple existence. I'm certain that a long life of experiences, good and bad, had brought them to be where they were, and in their own simple way, they had found contentment.

2

What Is Home?

When I hear the word "home," comfort comes to mind. I think of peace and tranquility, a place to belong, a place where meals are enjoyed together, where family is celebrated and nurturing takes place. A home is an inviting place to be. Everyone is accepted at home.

I don't suppose we have a perfect home. In fact, I *know* we don't. Yet as we continually work to improve our existence as a family, one thing we have been determined to do is to have people in our home, to open our door and kitchen table with genuine hospitality. During many of those visits over the years, I can remember a number of times, usually over a meal, when some of those friends and neighbors said they felt a sense of peace when they came to be with us, like there was some sort of calm that came over them. Perhaps it was based on comparing where they came from to how they felt sitting under our roof breaking bread at our table.

Sadly, home has never been a place of safety or peace for many. A lot of folks have such horrific memories of their growing up years that they never want to return or have anything to do with the relationships that were formed there. When you hear that old saying, "Home is where the heart is," you generally think of good things. But given the fact that the heart of a person can be developed by their environment and experiences, I expect a person's heart could be very warm, covered with scars, indifferent, or bitterly cold. It can vary greatly depending on the atmosphere of their upbringing.

I am fortunate and consider myself blessed to have been raised in a home and environment that was loving and nurturing, a place where I belonged, a place where I was taught the values of work, right and wrong, loving one another, and serving the Lord. Looking back on all my growing up years, if there was anything undesirable that came from those years, it was generally the result of my own poor choices, of *me* contributing negatively to our environment. Did I always like everything that was going on, like work, chores, and going to church every time the doors were open? Not exactly. But I know now most of what came from my home growing up moved me in a positive direction and charted my course in life toward success, not only financially, but more importantly, as the whole person I am.

An odd thing occurs when children are given the opportunity to express their artistic abilities during their early years. They cast their vision of what a home is by putting on paper a simple house with walls, a roof, windows, and a door right in the middle. Leading up to that front door might be a quaint little pathway lined with flowers on each side, along with a grassy yard.

On many a rooftop of those childhood masterpieces is affixed a chimney on one side with smoke curling up to the sky, representing a comfy fireplace inside, a place to warm your soul and put your feet up. The sun shines from the corner of the page with bright sunbeams, reaching out to scattered, puffy, white clouds across a deep-blue sky.

Certainly, that picture comes from our Western perspective, a product of our environment and upbringing, the culture from which our thoughts have been established. What about other parts of the world, such as Asia, Europe, Africa, South America, or Australia? While I've not travelled outside of North America, I suspect the concept of home is not much different wherever you lay your head. People want safety, shelter, and a place to rest their soul. They want to go to sleep knowing when they wake up the next day, things will be certain and well with their existence. But in so many instances, whether it's a mile or two down the road or clear across the globe, there are vast contrasts between comfort, contentment, peace, and tranquility and the ravages of poverty, war, and desperate loneliness.

A sound home does not necessarily have anything to do with wealth and riches or living in a hut with a dirt floor—it has everything to do with contentment: "Now godliness with contentment is great gain" (1 Timothy 6:6). Contentment can be a tricky state of mind, indeed. One person may say if you are content with what you have, you should live in a modest house and give everything else to the poor. While the modest home may be where some folks find themselves drawn for various reasons, others may live across the road from that modest home on a ranch that goes on for miles and miles. Each person has their place. Perhaps the ranch owner used to live in that modest home for a time, and as his hard work and success improved his lot in life, he moved up in the world, which allowed him to be the benefactor to the next person who may come along needing the same opportunity to improve. I believe God would have us be in a continuous state of improvement so as not to be a burden on our neighbors and the community. We should also be the ones who can find it in ourselves to open our hearts, wallet, or front door to give our neighbors a hand however God leads us. This is how we "love our neighbor as ourselves," as Jesus taught and demonstrated.

Given that God has children all over Planet Earth—His saints, His chosen people—it would be reasonable to say there may be a mystery to the mansions He has prepared for us when we arrive in our heavenly destination one day. Jesus gives us a picture of this heavenly realm in the gospel account from the book of John:

> *Let not your heart be troubled; you believe in God,*
> *believe also in Me. In My Father's house are many*
> *mansions; if it were not so, I would have told you.*
> *I go to prepare a place for you. And if I go and prepare*
> *a place for you, I will come again and receive you to*
> *Myself; that where I am, there you may be also.*
> *And where I go you know, and the way you know.*
> John 14:1-4

In this account, Jesus tells the disciples He is going away "to prepare a place" for them. During the time of this account, homes were quite different than many structures today. Even now, homes can come in a wide variety all over the globe, yet God has promised to prepare a place for us, a place of many mansions in which those of us who belong to Him will dwell. No matter the form these mansions or dwelling places take, we know Christ will receive us and welcome us into that fine place to live forever. It will be the grandest welcome and display of hospitality ever!

Now, as I've primarily been discussing the idea of home, let's not confuse that with the definition of a house. Simply put, a house is a structure, nothing more. It is designed to protect someone from the elements, and can be man-made, a cave in the side of a hill, or a gathering of sticks with straw affixed on top for a roof. That house becomes a home when someone moves in and settles there for a little while, or perhaps a long time, or a lifetime. As human nature sets in, most folks generally find themselves working to improve their place from the moment they set foot on the premises until they either move or vacate the property. I believe God gave most of us an innate desire to improve the state of our existence, not necessarily because we are unhappy with what we currently have (though that can be the case), but so that we can grow, increase, prosper, and be available to others in our journey through this life.

One person may say, "Well, just give me that little plot of land over there, along with a roof over my head and I'll be as content as a crawdad, living in my hole and minding my own business." The problem with that is that the good Lord said it is not good for mankind to be alone. Left to themselves, they become ... well, themselves. Inward-focused, the crawdad is always guarding its hole, remodeling its hole, and out hunting for food. While I'm no expert on crawdads, I've never seen them working together in a community, developing their existence, or being charitable to the crawdad across the field. What I have seen are crawdad skeletons, those individuals that, while working alone, became the victim of drought, flooding, or any manner of environmental catastrophe that can come and sweep them away. Not to mention they have nothing more to look forward to than to eat, sleep, swim, and dig.

Now, you must be wondering, *Where is he going with this?* I'm glad you asked.

You see, God, in all His magnificence, gave us longings. Yes, longings to improve, longings to procreate, longings to increase. And what's even better than all of that is a longing for the next life. Let me introduce you to a term that has become a part of my vocabulary in recent years. The word is "sojourner." No, that is not exactly a word used regularly in this day and time.

So, what exactly is a sojourner? Well, it's hard for a person in modern America to really understand this term since a great deal of our society is so inward and comfort focused. A sojourner is a person who is not settling for their existing circumstances but is on a journey to a place where their state of existence will vastly improve upon their arrival. While many people never want to get up to open the front door of their home and look outside, the sojourner is always standing on the porch, studying the horizon, and wondering, *Is it time to move on?* Sojourners are better compared to a nomadic culture of people who are always on the go, never really having a place to call home, and always looking elsewhere.

In the book of Philippians, Paul compares those who love the world as those people "who set their mind on earthly things" (Philippians 3:19). But he continues to say, "For our citizenship is in heaven, from which we also eagerly wait for the Savior, the Lord Jesus Christ" (Philippians 3:20). As believers in Jesus Christ, we have work to do here while at the same time working toward our future heavenly existence, in a continuous mindset of being ready to move. We should be packed and ready to go at all times so that when the moving van shows up, we are the first ones to load our things and head down the road.

Is home where our heart is? Indeed, it is. But think of the long game here, not the short term. While many of us may sense the smell of chocolate chip cookies our mom made when we hear the word "home," we would be much better off learning to think beyond our noses and stomachs, to a land God has prepared for those who love Him.

It's not the American Dream, or any earthly dream at all. It's God's future reality in a much better place!

3

The Birth of a Dream

In the latter part of the twentieth century, a ship set sail on what was supposed to be a never-ending, amazing voyage, one that would span years with no end in sight. As the years went by, the ship passed through treacherous waters and calm seas alike. Storms came and went, but the ship continued in the anticipation of greater days ahead and new lands to explore. At different ports along the way, the ship would dock, resupply, repair tattered sails, and embark on the journey once again. At times, a new passenger would join the ranks of those on board, thus increasing the size of the crew.

After leaving port one day with all on board refreshed and ready for the next long journey, the ship once again set sail for open seas. While that leg of the trip began much the same as so many others, a few days into the voyage, a storm was spotted on the horizon. As usual, the crew prepared for the worst. But this was no ordinary storm. Tempestuous winds began to beat down on the ship. Waves crashed over the deck, nearly washing those on board out to sea. Tossed to and fro, the crew began hurling the cargo into the sea to lighten the load in hopes of riding the storm out to safety. As lightning streaked across the expanse of the black night sky, it revealed a strip of land in the distance. The crew had little choice but to try to run the ship aground.

After no small effort to save the ship and those on board, everyone braced themselves for the inevitable crash as they struck a coral reef, bursting the ship and its cargo into splintering ruins. With nothing else to do but swim for their lives, the crew grabbed hold of what they could and made their way to the shore. Despite the ship being a total loss, all on board escaped with their lives and gathered on the land. Gasping for breath, bewildered, and broken, they huddled on the beach, waiting for the long night to come to an end.

As the storm began to pass and the sunrise emerged on the horizon, bringing a fresh, new day, the crew watched the bits and pieces of what they had invested their lives in drift out to sea, never to be seen again. The beach was littered with unrecognizable fragments of things they once possessed. From that devastated beach, life had to begin anew. As the crew gathered themselves and their senses, it was at that point they determined it was time to set sail in different, separate directions.

I Had Lost Nearly Everything

In my late twenties, the shipwreck of divorce blew my world apart. An explosion went off like a bomb, leaving a crater in my life and an endless task of picking up the pieces and putting them back together. As far as I was concerned, I would never marry again. I was done. I was in a constant state of numbness, regularly asking God why it had happened. I walked away from that experience with my faith in God, my two beautiful children, and my job, but had to start over when it came to a place to live and personal possessions. Dad and Mom never left my side, as well as my church family, who put their arms around me and carried me daily. Was this my new existence, *my* American Dream? It seemed more like a nightmare.

After the devastation, the two kids and I settled into an apartment for a short time. If there was ever anything I wanted after the divorce, it was my kids. I had God, my church, family, and friends to cling to, but my kids were my life. Possessions meant nothing to me. While the kids split their time between their mother's house and where I lived, I wanted to do all I could to provide stability for them whenever they were with me. Before long, the apartment life grew old and I began looking for a place the kids and I could call home. In short order, we settled into a modest two-bedroom house in a quiet neighborhood.

I didn't take my sights off that little house once we were planted there. As we settled in, we enjoyed the nice above-ground pool, the deck, and the luxurious carpet-like grass in the backyard. We determined to repair anything that needed fixing on the house. My dad and mom helped me a lot when they came to see us. Mom looked after the kids and fed us while Dad and I worked on various minor projects or things that needed fixing or updating. I learned for the first time how to be a pool cleaner— and how much I hated it. Yet we enjoyed that pool immensely that summer. Although I hadn't been looking for one or desiring it, God had a way of giving us that pool, a bonus that came with the property, to help us forget all the sorrow and difficulty we had been through.

It's funny how you settle into a groove in life at times and just get to thinking, *Well, this is it. This will always be my lot in life.* Time has a way of healing you, growing you, and allowing you to adjust your vision for the future. Although I had no intention of moving on from that house or seeking a new relationship, God moved me in miraculous ways, calling me to more, teaching me to stop settling for one thing when He had something much better. Praise the Lord that He still moves, then and now.

Soon, God brought me to a place of healing and to a place where I met another victim of the shipwreck that is divorce. In our little town, not too far from where I lived, was a lovely, sweet lady whom I had never met. She was a native of our town, born and raised there, and through similar circumstances, had come to be a single parent like me. Then God brought us together miraculously. Another storm had arrived in my life, but this time in a good way, one that God used to bring hope and encouragement to me, which I desperately needed. God sent a sweet little blue-eyed storm into my life to swoop me up and help me see there was more in my future, so much more.

Nearly a year went by like a blur. It was one of the most exciting times of my life as I grew to know my future wife, Miss Katrina. The following spring, almost a year after we had met, we brought our two little families together in an amazing wedding ceremony that blessed us all. Katrina's boys were the candle lighters, my son was the ring bearer, and my daughter was the flower girl. At the end of our ceremony, our pastor had us all hold hands in a circle and prayed a blessing over our new family. Thus began our adventure, together with God. It has been an exhilarating ride ever since!

Once my sweet Katrina and I were happily married, choosing where to live was a no-brainer. My little two-bedroom, one-bath house was out of the question. It would have to go. Katrina's house was a new, brick, three-bedroom, two-bath house she was very proud of. If it was perfect for her, it would be perfect for me. Even when our family size doubled and we brought our children together, it was all the space six people would ever need.

A couple of years into our marriage, God blessed us with our first son together, Bradley, which brought our family size to seven. No problem, we could manage that. Two years later, our daughter Hannah arrived on the scene, bringing our total to eight. Before the arrival of Hannah, we had promised the Lord we would trust Him with our family size, which, given our fertility track record and young ages, could mean many more children to come.

We came up with a plan to turn half of our two-car garage into a bedroom for the boys, thus opening space in another bedroom to establish a nursery and girls' room. That worked out nicely, giving us much-needed space for the time being.

After Hannah's arrival, God kept blessing us like clockwork: we became pregnant with another child. Our house that had been fine for our family when we married was rapidly getting smaller and smaller, seemingly bursting at the seams. What were we to do?

We turned to God's Word, where He pointed out to us what it says in the book of Proverbs: "Where there is no counsel, the people fall; but in the multitude of counselors there is safety" (Proverbs 11:14).

Indeed, we had heard that verse before, having been in church most of our lives, but God put a special emphasis on it for us at that time, leading us to see the value of that oh-so-important concept. God reminded us that when you are making important decisions about the future of your family, it is good to lean on those who have already been down the path on which you are about to set foot.

While we knew a lot of folks in our church and had certainly sought the advice of our parents many times in the past, it seemed fitting to reach out to some of our mature church members, those whom we knew had a reputation in our church and the community for making wise choices, those who had gone before us and learned so much along the way. We chose two older couples whom we had come to know, along with a sweet widow whose family had been vital to our church and community for many years. They all seemed honored that we invited them to have a meal with us and asked to glean their godly knowledge and wisdom. One of the key things to look for in seeking godly advice is to know that the people you are receiving from are those you can trust, those who have your best interest in mind, and above all, those who have God's desires for you in mind.

We should always be very careful in seeking clear direction, as the heart can be deceitfully wicked when it is not in alignment with God's holy ways. In the Old Testament, after King Solomon (the wisest man who ever lived) died, his son Rehoboam was crowned king over all of Israel. When King Rehoboam sought advice, he chose to reject the wise counsel of the elders and instead followed his wicked heart and listened to his immature friends, who had no interest in doing what was right. That led to disaster, resulting in wars all the days of his reign until his death. Yes, we should be very careful not to gather around us those who will only tell us what our itching ears long for. God knows the intent of our hearts and will reward us accordingly.

During our fellowship meal, we presented our challenges to those godly followers of Christ. After much discussion, we boiled our options down to four possibilities: we could add space onto our existing home, move to an existing larger house, look for property and build a larger house, or do nothing and make the best of our current circumstances.

Because we had such limits on what we could do to our existing home, one of which was the small size of our city lot, we quickly set that idea aside. Doing nothing—the ostrich approach of sticking our heads in the sand and pretending everything would be okay—was just not feasible either. After a very fruitful discussion, our godly advisors unanimously agreed moving was the right thing for our family, whether that meant buying an existing home that would work or building a new one on some property we had yet to obtain. Either way, we had options. As we leaned on the "multitude of counselors" God had surrounded us with, as well as both our parents, we felt good that the decision we were making was based on sound judgment and not just our own limited experience and ignorance.

That fateful meal put us on a winding path in search of elsewhere.

4

A Hill to Call Home

M any times, when looking for something specific to purchase, I have the mindset that if I don't hurry and buy what I've found, someone else will come along and snatch it out from under me before I can return. While there is something to be said for market timing, I tend to think that when I see something of value, the whole world is already watching, or will be soon, and it will be gone if I do not act. In some situations, particularly with purchasing a vehicle, I have had to train my thoughts and emotions to stop, pause, and remember that this is not the last car in the world, and if someone else gets it, they probably needed it worse than I did. Fear and emotions are generally not good contributors to sound money decisions.

When Katrina and I made the decision to begin looking for either a larger house or a property to build a house on, we made it a high priority, taking advantage of every spare moment we had to load the kids in the van and check out places we had researched.

The kids, especially the older ones, seemed to enjoy going into houses to look around, checking things out and exploring every square inch of any place we scoped out. At times it was challenging, as we wanted to make the most of looking at a property while at the same time ensuring the kids were safe and within a reasonable distance. Eventually, the property hunting wore on us all, but nonetheless, we pressed on, packing everyone along for the adventures that occurred almost every weekend.

Two houses in our small town seemed like they could be the right size for us, but they were both very old and odd. They had been built nearly a century ago during a time when everyone in town had at least a half-dozen kids, much the same as our family size. One thing that stood out about those places was they both had creepy-looking cellars with dirt floors, like something you would see in an old, scary movie where they lock people up and leave them for dead. In addition to that, one of those houses shared the driveway with the funeral home next door. I'm sure it could have been a fine home for someone, but something didn't seem right about having a bird's-eye view of every funeral that occurred in town and every dead body that came and went. We marked those off the list. Too old, too close to neighbors, too creepy, and not enough exposure to country living.

We soon came across a property on a gentle hillside with dirt-road access. While the road was not especially desirable, it could work. We wandered all over that seven-acre lot, which was nicely wooded, and I pictured where we could bring in a driveway and a place to build a house. After much deliberation with a reputable homebuilder we had begun working with, along with the landowner who had the property for sale, we determined the land did not have adequate drainage for a septic system. This would have meant building a more elaborate system that would be very costly. We spent some money on the front end to investigate that deal and clarify what was needed: it turned out to be money well spent that saved us potentially thousands down the road. Regretfully, we marked that property off the list. While we loved the location and the wooded environment, it just didn't make financial sense to spend nearly as much for a septic system as we would have spent for the land itself.

Things were stalling. We needed something affordable, yet we needed a location that would keep our two oldest boys in the same school district they had been in for years. We were becoming discouraged, and waiting was wearing us down. In the process, however, we were learning a lot along the way; we were picking up on many things about building our own home. Ideally, we had been set on hiring a general contractor to build us the turnkey house we longed for, one that we would do minimal to no work on. We just didn't seem to think that my work schedule (or our birthing schedule!) could handle the stress of us building our own home. But God knew we could handle more.

In the spring of every year, I was accustomed to being off work on Good Friday, a nice perk that came with the employer I had been working for. So, on Good Friday 2004, we set out to identify some lots for sale in the city limits, something we hadn't considered before. Because living out in the country was all our brains had been focused on, we had ruled out anything that would be available within the city limits of our small town. We looked at several lots, but nothing seemed to look like anything that could work for us.

Then we stumbled onto something. In a somewhat secluded part of town, off the beaten path, was a small subdivision that had never been completed. It had been started years earlier, but had met with limited success due to the challenging, hilly lots. At the time we considered the property, there were still a significant number of lots available, and only a few houses speckled among the lots. Then we discovered the lots on one side of the road bordered the hundred-acre city park property, a mostly undeveloped, wooded mountain that hadn't been used to its full potential, except for the small city park at the top of the mountain.

Studying the land plat, I saw most of the lots were about half an acre, while a couple of them were almost twice the size. There was one large lot that bordered the creek near the bottom of the hill, and the largest lot was up on the hill, bordering the city property. While we had dreamed of building near a creek, that lot didn't seem quite right, and existing neighbors were too close. So, we wandered up the hill to the one surrounded by forest, in the heart of the subdivision, bordering the hundred-acre wood.

I could see it right away. Although the place seemed to be just a wild, overgrown, woolly mess, I could see the potential. I began scoping things out, visualizing a house nestled in the middle of the tall trees, along with a winding driveway that would have to be carved out of the hillside to get us up and down the hill. Every tree we could possibly keep would stay to create our little heaven on earth right there in the middle of town. I could see it, but Katrina could not. Thus was the beginning of many, many conversations of me carefully and patiently showing my sweet bride how things would look and where they would be. I envisioned it. I could see it. This was it. That untouched, undiscovered, and overgrown jungle could soon be a place to call our home!

Now, all we had to do was snatch it up before someone found out what we had discovered. If the secret about that place was discovered, it would be a feeding frenzy of rabid, senseless home-buyers (like us), falling over each other with sacks of cash. We later learned it wasn't like that at all, not even close, but nonetheless, we quickly made an offer on the property that was accepted by the seller, and we proceeded to close on the sale. Because we had been saving up for that event, we had a reasonable sum of cash to bring to the table, but we learned that loaning money for land was something banks cringe about. While we could have proceeded with a bank loan to top off our available funds, we came up with some creative financing of our own and were able to close the deal quite soon. So, in the spring of 2004, we glee-fully became the owners of our very own acre of land, the little piece of heaven we had longed for.

Although we knew it going into the deal, we were soon reminded that land ownership requires work, at least if you want to develop it into something useful and of value. We didn't care. That was exciting for us, a chance to go and play on something that was our very own. We were soon having workdays on the property since it was just a short drive from our current home. On many of those workdays, we would have a campfire inside a ring of rocks we had built. We would gather around, have weenie roasts, and enjoy the excitement of our new place, our home away from home. I had also learned that three teenage boys would do an awful lot of work if I provided them pizza. I was certain to take full advantage of the cheap labor!

In June of that year, I learned that my body did, in fact, have limitations. Still in my mid-thirties, I would go over to the property and work like crazy, ignoring the heat, humidity, critters, and whatever else came my way. One day, it got the best of me.

While I had grown up in Arkansas and cleared all manner of brush in my early years alongside my dad, I never remember a time when poison ivy gave me any trouble. Ticks, chiggers, and mosquitoes, maybe—but not poison ivy.

I was working and working, pulling vines from trees, piling up briars for burning, and getting the lot ready for the home we hadn't even designed yet. Then one evening, after coming back from brush clearing, getting cleaned up, and going to bed, it began … the itching.

Never in my life had I experienced a poison ivy outbreak. But at that moment, my thirty-five years of missing out on that poisonous, silent attacker caught up to me. I was in misery. I took hot showers, cold baths, and held my arms under scalding hot water in the kitchen sink. I applied baking soda, anti-itch creams, antihistamines, and all manner of other salves and solutions. Nothing worked. In the middle of one of the most humid and hot months of our year, I had the worst case of poison ivy on both arms known to mankind. I couldn't sleep, which led to me not being able to focus on work. Everything we researched about poison ivy said that it would eventually pass with enough time. Evidently, "enough time" had yet to pass.

After a couple of weeks in sheer misery (I'm itching just thinking about it), I decided to go to the doctor to see what concoction they had in their arsenal to end my self-induced torture. That visit ended with a poke in my backside—a steroid shot. I reluctantly left the doctor, hoping things would improve quickly. Things did not improve. They worsened. In addition to me having bleeding, itching sores from the poison ivy, I broke out with hives all over my body as it rejected the intrusion of the steroid shot. Now I was itching all over. To make a long story short, I just had to suck it up, stick it out, and wait for it to pass. It eventually did—two weeks later.

That hot, humid summer was the time to let the ground (and ourselves) rest for a while and pursue an eagerly anticipated weeklong vacation we had planned earlier in the year. Additionally, Katrina was quite pregnant with another daughter, who was scheduled to arrive in just a few weeks toward the end of August. Our getaway provided exciting and memorable family time and was exactly the break we needed right after our land development work and prior to the birth of our daughter.

The heat of August came and went, but not without the special arrival of our sweet little Holly, a blessing from the Lord. Soon thereafter, as Holly settled into our family life, we renewed our focus on our plans to build our dream house, which was becoming increasingly important to us as each day passed. We would have our house on the hill, one way or another, all in good time.

5

The House That God Built

Go confidently in the direction of your dreams,
live the life you've imagined.
Henry David Thoreau

As I write the words of this chapter, I am sitting inside a room that was built with my own two hands, an office specifically designed for this very purpose—to think, to write, to meditate on God's Word, to pray, and to use the gifts God has given me. The ceramic tile under my feet, which my chair is sitting on, was put down by me and my son Bradley, who is developing and pursuing his talents as well. Years ago, I had no idea how to lay tile, hammer a nail, cut a board, or do a plethora of other things required to get by in this life. Some of it I can do well, other things not so much. I am still honing my skills and still have a lot to learn about most everything. But I *can* do things, by the grace of God.

"'Can't' never did anything," my dad would often tell me. I will never forget those words that ring as true today as they did in my early years. When I would say I was unable to do something, Dad was always there to let me know I could, in fact, do all manner of things. He didn't leave me to myself to figure it out alone; he would be there to teach me what he knew or to learn something alongside me as we worked together. I will always be grateful for his persistence to push through, get things done, and encourage me to do the same.

Breaking Ground

*And they labor in vain who build the house,
unless the Lord builds it.*
Psalm 127:1

We had prayed for this moment, waited on God for it, sought a multitude of counselors, and had everything in alignment. In addition to God giving us the green light to build a house, we had also clearly heard from Him to trust Him with our family size. That meant more children: our seventh had just arrived. Although our older children had been lovingly accepting of each new brother or sister that came along and of our calling to bring more children into the world, the house we were living in was getting smaller and smaller every day. The walls seemed to be moving in. A sense of urgency was upon us.

In all our journeys looking for land on which to build a house, as well as looking at houses to buy, we had collected a pile of information, books, pictures, and raw ideas about what we desired in a house. We would go to the library, check out as many house plan books as we could carry, bring them home, and flip, flip, flip through them, bookmarking every page we found that looked like something we wanted. Our family of nine was on a mission to create a dream house.

While looking for land and communicating with turnkey home builders, we eventually learned it would be very expensive to hire someone to build the house we desired. We would either have to shrink our house size, cut back on amenities, or develop another plan. We had already purchased and cleaned up our property, so we were somewhat locked into the limitations of the lot size and topography. The logical conclusion was to build a two-story house with a walk-out basement into the hillside. We were discouraged that we could not afford the turnkey route, since we wanted to lean heavily on their expertise. Our mindset needed an adjustment.

Given our busy lifestyle with all our children and activities, we originally thought building a house was out of our reach. However, after no small effort in seeking counsel from friends who had built homes or were currently in the process, and knowing both of our parents were one hundred percent onboard, we determined that I would be the general contractor. I had built a doghouse or two by that point in my life, so building a human house was just on a larger scale, right? In addition to the moral support of our family and friends, our two dads committed to helping us do whatever was needed to get the project off the ground and to the finish line. That was huge!

Being a drafter by trade, I wanted to do all the design work myself, but I was a mechanical drafter, not an architectural drafter. I was used to drawing machine parts, not house plans. However, I did have a flare for creativity and tinkered with it enough that I could lay my vision out for Katrina, study our house design books, and get to where we needed to be. We spent hours poring over those books from the library and dragging the kids along every Sunday afternoon for months, taking photos inside open houses. If we were ever driving anywhere and saw a house with some feature we were looking for, we would stop and take pictures. We even met several homeowners in the building process, always explaining to them why we were staring at their houses. On one occasion, we went to look at an old two-story farmhouse in the country, and upon our arrival in the driveway, the lady who lived there invited us in and gave us a tour of the place. You just never know how nice people can be until you ask!

In the design process, as we were learning about what would fit into the footprint we had to work with, our designer was very helpful. She was straightforward and made many recommendations along the way to help us get most everything under our roof we desired. Somewhere in those discussions, as we tried to fit everything into two levels, we realized we weren't satisfied with the sizes of rooms and the limitations we were working with. I suppose we could have made every bedroom tiny, like contractors do in low budget spec homes. But we had already experienced those small rooms in several places we had lived, so we wanted to improve our living space for everyone.

To get us moving in a new direction and out of our two-story mindset, our designer suggested increasing the roof pitch significantly, raising the peak of the roof, and adding a third floor and second staircase. That would add two bedrooms on either end of the third floor, along with another bathroom in between. It would also open floor space on the second story to make the bedrooms the sizes we desired. After readjusting the plans, we had the number of rooms we wanted and the size we wanted—without changing the foundation size one bit.

Then I paused, having one of those flashback moments. I could see those times when I was a boy, the one who had dreamed of owning a three-story house. We were now on our way, completing the plans and ready to begin *building* that three-story house I had dreamed about.

When you're thinking about all the features you want in a home, in addition to all the basic things to create a shelter from the elements, the budget can be a troublesome friend at the party. Yes, we had our list of wants and desires to go along with the necessities required to build a functioning home. Nevertheless, the bank wanted to see a plan, especially one with a budget. My precisionist nature and desire for things to come out perfectly, especially regarding the money estimates, was a hindrance in moving forward. My father-in-law, having been through the process himself, gave me a bit of sage advice about that challenging estimation exercise. He said, "Whatever you come up with for an estimate, add ten to fifteen percent and you might be close." When going through the process, that was hard to see, especially for a novice. But in the end, I saw it very plainly. He was right.

Going into building the house, we knew it was going to be what seemed like an impossible task, a mountain we could not climb. Those are the moments that define a person. When adversity comes and you are put to the test, what you are made of rises to the top. In addition to looking deep inside yourself to persevere, it is crucial to know when you must lean on God and the community He has placed around you to accomplish the great things He has called you to do. God has a wonderful way of surrounding you with just the right people at just the right time, messengers sent on an errand on His behalf. What's so interesting is that those people and circumstances can all be intertwined into your life in such a way that most of them, if not all, have no idea they are being used for God's purpose.

We all have our ups and downs as each day of life passes by. I can remember a day not long ago when I found myself in a place of discouragement, feeling like nobody else on the planet even knew I existed anymore, just having one of my little pity parties. The Enemy of our souls has a way of using those moments to grind us down and beat us into a pulp. Yet that old rascal the Devil forgets every time whom he is dealing with.

Just when I was feeling down and out, God had another plan. He had an old friend call me out of the blue whom I'd not heard from in a while. I answered the phone and was instantly encouraged. Later that afternoon, I ran into another friend of ours in the store we'd not seen in a long time. Again, encouragement. That same evening, my old boss from work called me just to catch up and see how I was doing. The next couple of days were the same: I kept hearing from people—not just ordinary people, but ones with whom I would not normally be in contact in my day-to-day activities. I carried on, encouraged that God had put a host of people around me who knew me, loved me, and wanted God's best for my life. He is such a good Father!

Now that we had our solid house plans in hand, the winter of that year was spent lining up contractors, finalizing the bank financing, and setting a timeline to begin. While it would have been better to start when it was dryer, given that winter and spring in our area are the wettest times of year, we wanted to push forward as soon as possible. So, on March 15, 2005, we broke ground on our new home.

There was no fanfare at the groundbreaking, but we were certainly rejoicing in our hearts. We did not make the front page of the newspaper, nor did the mayor show up with his spray-painted gold shovel. It was the day when heavy equipment arrived, when our first and most important contractor began the foundation work. We really wanted the foundation done right, which meant we had waited a long time for those guys to show up, a reputable family crew who did major excavation and serious concrete work in our area. They had come highly recommended, and they didn't disappoint.

Sometimes, when you pray and ask the Lord for things and live in the expectation of those things happening, you can forget about time and that the rest of the world is still operating around you. You get lost in the moment. We had been told by multiple contractors and friends that this project would take a minimum of six months to complete. We had friends who were currently dealing with their subcontractors not showing up at their house or delays that went from days to weeks. We prayed against that happening, asking God to line up everything to perfection, that people would exceed our expectations and keep the house moving along at a record pace.

I never remember a time during the process when we had delays. On many, many days we had multiple contractors falling over each other to get their work done. It was seemingly unheard of, but God had brought an army of workers to our place to get that house up.

My Turn to Work

Now, being the general contractor (while working my full-time job), I had amazing intentions of documenting the entire event from start to finish, from groundbreaking to move-in. That started well, with me taking pictures as I went by the site after work every day to check on things and the progress taking place. But my good intentions to document the entire event on camera was short lived. As I became very busy with working on the house myself, taking pictures became the furthest thing from my mind.

Part of being the general contractor meant figuring out who would do the things we hadn't hired anyone else to do. That meant lots of work opportunities for both of our dads and anyone else who could pitch in and help, especially me. Sometimes it worked well to do certain things on our own to save the money, but at other times, it did not.

Right after the foundation guys had completed their work and left us with an amazing concrete floor and very tall, solid concrete walls for the back of the basement, it was time to backfill the wall before the framing crew showed up. That seemed like an opportunity to save some money, especially since we had three very strong teenage boys who worked for pizza and knew how to operate a shovel. So that's what we set out to do.

The work commenced. With all the boys and me, shovels in hand, we could surely move the huge mountains of dirt piled up behind the basement walls and fill in that monstrous hole in no time flat—at least, that's what I envisioned. It went well at first, but the piles of dirt, no matter how hard we tried, just didn't seem to move into that giant, bottomless cavern as fast as we thought it would. We shoveled and shoveled, and as time went on and days passed, I could see that it was one of those not-so-bright moments in my new house-building experience. The framing crew would arrive soon, and we could not have all this dirt standing in their way causing delays. When all our muscles ached and cramped with pain, it was time to call our bulldozer buddy and spend some money to get the excavation completed. Thankfully, he was available and came to relieve us of our shoveling duties. It was a lesson learned and money well spent for certain!

I still have a briefcase full of the notes, receipts, invoices, and other paraphernalia I collected along the way in getting that house up and operational. As I said before, I had amazing *intentions* of documenting the process well. After the framing crew came in after the foundation guys had left, things began moving rather quickly. Instead of hiring a traditional "stick builder" framing crew, we hired a company that brought in prefabricated wall frames, upper flooring, and trusses. Within a few weeks, we had gone from a wooded forest plot to three levels of wood framing that touched the sky.

Building the house you've been dreaming about for years takes you to emotions you can't imagine. There were several moments in the construction of the house that really seemed surreal, that made me stop, look around, and think, *Wow, this is really happening!* I can remember one day in particular...

When the framers had only been there for a few days, I came over from work on a beautiful April afternoon to see all three levels practically complete, except for the roof. That included the two roughed-in staircases that were in place. As I drove up the hill, admiring the work that had been done, I couldn't help but notice the sheer height of the structure, as if the stairs had been built to the sky and the forest was trying to reach to Heaven. It took me no time at all to walk inside, scale the two flights of stairs in awe, and arrive all the way to the top to the location that would soon be our third-floor balcony overlooking the vaulted entryway.

Honestly, it was kind of scary. With only a few two-by-fours nailed on to create a makeshift rail, my heart was pounding with excitement and fear of heights at the same time. It was exhilarating to look out across the tree line, into the valley below, and above to the blue sky, knowing we had dreamed about this place and it was coming together so quickly. I was so very excited!

Shortly after the framing was done, the roofer arrived, and before we knew it, we had our house in the dry. The Lord had done His part in providing amazing weather to that point, especially given the spring's rainy tendencies. The plumber, electrician, and HVAC guys were ready to get busy, as were the insulation crew, sheetrock installers, and sheetrock finishers. Everything was rolling along with amazing precision.

Having a contractor build a turnkey house did not leave room for getting the best deal on things like light fixtures and tile. But I was the general contractor who called the shots. Long before we broke ground on the house, Katrina and I had developed a knack for bargain hunting for finish materials. We were going to have to spend a lot of time at home stores to pick out those materials anyway, so we might as well save a bundle in the process. We had been packing the garage full at our current home until nothing more could fit. There were stacks of tile, bathroom fixtures, lights, and all manner of odds and ends for finishing the house. Once, we even drove out to a field in the country and stood in the back of a guy's semi-trailer to buy oak stair rails for ten cents on the dollar. We were piecing the house together as we went, but we were making it happen. I can remember many, many trips from the store with my little four-door 1998 Honda Civic loaded to capacity. It's amazing what you can get in one of those cars when you fold the seats down and lay boards all the way up into the windshield!

With our two dads and I being the main crew to fill in the labor gaps, we set to work painting, doing trim work, building staircases and stair rails, hanging doors, laying tile, and no telling what else. One of the best investments I made in the process was an airless paint sprayer, which allowed me to blow through five-gallon buckets of paint like nobody's business.

One day, when the sheetrock finishers had completed their job and it was time for me to paint, we faced the dilemma of not having scaffolds to paint the high parts of the entryway. Then as they were about to leave, the sheetrock guys asked if they could leave their scaffolds there for the weekend until they could pick them up.

Thinking quickly, I said, "Sure, but would you mind if I used them until you return?" to which they replied, "No problem." In addition to them leaving the scaffolds, they had also left all the windows masked off, which saved me from having to do it myself. God was so good to put so many little things like that together for us, things that just made the process so seamless.

In addition to all our subcontractors working so faithfully, at several opportune times we had friends, family, and church family come to help out along the way. Even though the sun was beating down on our place and the bricklayers and siding installers were taking the brunt of the summer heat, things kept clicking along at record pace. I think the only person who caused delays was the city building inspector, who would show up at times to let us know that a stair rail was not just right or that something was out of place. But for the most part, those things were minor and ensured we had a properly built house that exceeded the building codes.

My fear of heights was put to the test on that house construction. Early in the process, as the roofers completed their job, my dad, who was helping me oversee and install the chimney pipes for the fireplace, told me to take a rope, crawl up on the roof, and measure how tall the outside frame of the chimney was from the ground. I thought that sounded like an easy enough task, so I took our ladder, which was a bit too short, and hopped up on the roof from the backyard, where the roof was closer to the ground. I had to crawl up carefully, given the exceedingly steep roof pitch, but I did it. I made my way over to the chimney, which was at the edge of the highest point of the third story, and then I made the mistake of looking down.

Yikes! I froze.

All alone on the job site, and long before everyone carried cell phones, I was stuck there in the heat of the day, clinging to the chimney frame for dear life. Eventually, after talking to God and myself for a while, I told God that if He would get me off that roof, I would never get back on it again. He gave me the courage to crawl down off of that roof, dangle my feet off the side to reach the ladder that was nowhere near tall enough, and shimmy down. God did His part, so I did mine. I never climbed on that roof again, ever.

Later in the building process I did, however, get to assist my dad, the chimney pipe expert and installer. I constructed and crawled up scaffolds one at a time, handing him pieces of pipe that he assembled all the way to the top. I had a frozen moment up on the scaffolds as well, and when I did, Dad was sure to share some wonderful stories of how he had climbed up masts on Navy ships in years past to change out or repair electrical equipment. Dad said during some of those times when they were at sea, he would be out over the water, at the top of the mast, swinging back and forth like a pendulum.

In Dad's mind, I later learned, I must have seemed like the guy in the Navy they referred to as the Jolly Green Giant. Let me explain. During the Vietnam War, Dad was overseeing the repair of antennae equipment on a Navy destroyer. He instructed a guy who had a size-sixteen shoe and seemed like he was seven feet tall, whom they jokingly referred to as the Jolly Green Giant. Well, apparently Mr. Giant was comfortable with his own height, but when he was about halfway up the antennae mast, he froze and could go no farther. Dad had to climb up the mast and coach him down, one rung at a time, until his massive feet were back on deck. Yep, that was me, so very happy to be on the ground after scaling those scaffolds. That little chimney pipe assembly job seemed like a cakewalk to Dad, even at the age of sixty-eight.

Shortly after groundbreaking, Katrina excitedly shared the news with me that we were again pregnant. Knowing our eighth child would be arriving later in the year expedited things, making us work even faster. The endless days we spent working nonstop on the house seemed to run together in a blur. God put an unbelievable cast together to get that place up and gave us a strength we didn't know we had. The house was a growing testimony to what God could do through us if we were obedient to follow the dreams He gave us. We obeyed, and He surely blessed us for it.

Yes, we did things we thought we could never do. We learned so very much. Our friends and family were so generous in their support of us along the way. We did it all without running out of money. And the best part was on August 12, 2005, in just under five months' time, when all mankind had told us it would take six months or longer, we moved into our dream house, God's house. We could not have done it without Him. Our God was so very faithful to help us through it all.

We were so thankful to God that He helped us build that house in such a timely and unforgettable way. For years, we meant to create a nice plaque near our front entryway, like you see at a historical monument or park, with dates, details, and the heading: The House That God Built. Unfortunately, life has a way of getting away from us, and the plaque was never created. Nonetheless, we are forever grateful to our Lord for all He did to bless us and amaze us through that house.

6

No Place Like Home

We had taken a turn off the beaten path for certain, and with God's amazing guidance and provision, we had built the house of our dreams on the side of the hill. But shortly thereafter, the first house payment was due. Then another payment was due, and then another. And this would continue for the next thirty years, month after month, until the house no longer belonged to the bank, but to us. Our shackles of debt were firmly affixed to our hands and feet. At the rate we were going, we would finish paying the house off right before we applied for Social Security. And, to top it all off, our payment was about twice as much as we were paying on our other house, for which we were also still paying a mortgage. Yikes! We needed to get out from under our old house and its mortgage before we were buried in all that debt! The storm of two mortgages did not last too long, however. In a few short months, we were able to find a buyer for our old house, move on, and put our focus on our new baby boy who would soon be arriving.

In no time at all, life was back to some sort of normal and we began enjoying the fruits of our labor. Shortly after moving into our new home, Katrina was working diligently to get us settled and preparing for the birth of Joshua, while at the same time caring for our three youngest children, who were by now four years, two and a half years, and fifteen months old. When she wasn't pouring herself into caring for those little bundles of joy, we were very active with our four oldest children, ages sixteen, fifteen, thirteen, and ten. She was always a very busy lady while I was away for work each day.

If there is ever a path to follow, Katrina has a knack for abandoning it and setting her feet on ground where no foot has stepped. On one unseasonably warm day in November, not long before Thanksgiving, Katrina struck out up the mountain behind our home, leading Bradley and Hannah as she carried little Holly atop her very large stomach. They had a time of it in the woods, cutting their own path as they worked their way up the steep incline to the crest of the hill where the city park sat. Emerging at the top, they played at the playground for a while, then returned home for lunch and a restful afternoon. When I returned home from work that evening and learned about Katrina's adventurous day, I reminded her of all the things that could have happened to her with three toddlers and one more child virtually in the birth canal. Did any of my common-sense comments deter Ms. Perseverance? Of course not.

Our youngest son, Joshua, arrived in mid-December. Joshua's birth was another one of our many miracles. After complications from our previous two pregnancies, the attending doctor had told us we should cease having children. We chose to listen to God instead, ignoring her advice. The result was a perfectly delivered baby boy, no complications whatsoever, whom we brought home from the hospital on the following day. The celebration of our miracle baby boy gave us a special reason to celebrate Christmas that year, our first Christmas in our house on the hill. Life was good, and we loved our new home and growing family!

One of the reasons we were so drawn to building our house on the hill, aside from providing ourselves some much-needed space, was to be able to provide our children with a place to call home, a home that belonged to us all, a place where we could start a new chapter in life together. We had been working at being a blended family for years, but we had never been able to call a place home that was new to all of us, a fresh beginning.

Not long after the arrival of Joshua, we had the privilege of experiencing our first spring on the hill. We had grown used to the spectacular winter view across the valley through our leafless trees. But as spring blossomed, one of our favorite seasons of the year, we saw the beautiful transformation of God bringing our hill to life, covering our new home in a veil of green as the trees came alive.

Although our home was pristine and new on the inside, the outside landscaping still required a great deal of work to get it up to presentable condition. One of our first projects was to build a flower bed along the sidewalk that connected the driveway to our wraparound front porch. The sidewalk had a substantial drop-off around the edge, which raised our concerns about our smaller children playing on it and falling, so we built a very nice retaining wall just below the sidewalk, complete with the flower bed.

With every home we have lived in, all we ever needed was some dirt and time for my sweet wife to bring things to life with flowers, shrubs, and all manner of living things. She is certainly gifted in that area. Now that I had done my part at getting the flower bed ready, it was time to turn Katrina loose with her skills of planting flowers. While she was working on that, I decided to find a small ornamental tree that would look great in the middle of our new flower bed, giving anyone who came for a visit a grand welcome.

One of the blessings of living on our hillside full of trees had been enjoying all the dogwoods blooming every year, so I decided to try and find one of the smaller dogwoods and transplant it to the flower bed. Dogwoods were very special to Katrina and me because our joyous honeymoon was spent at a lovely cottage in the spring, surrounded by blooming dogwoods in every direction.

I searched long and hard through the woods behind our home and finally settled on the perfect candidate for the flower bed. I carefully set to work, digging up the largest root ball possible and transporting it to its new home. We gently packed it in, watered it well, then stood back and admired our crown jewel as its beautiful white blooms lit up the entrance to our home.

It didn't take long for the dogwood tree to show signs of sadness from its move as it soon began wilting, which is not uncommon when transplanting trees. We became worried when it did not appear to bounce back. After a long, hot summer, the tree just didn't seem to make it at all, and its tiny limbs dried up, along with the few leaves it attempted to hang on to. As fall came along and the limbs became brittle, indicating that it was likely a goner, we cut the tree down to a stump about a foot above the ground, thinking we would get another tree the following year.

Another winter beat down on us, and we forgot about flowers and trees for a while, and then spring arrived once again: time to plant flowers and begin tree shopping. Although our budget was tight, we decided we needed to get a nice tree from a local nursery. But to our surprise, our little dogwood that had received such a horrendous amputation in the fall began to show some signs of life, sprouting some new limbs. As its gangly twigs reached for the sky, it looked scraggly, but we decided to give it a chance to see what it would become. Although it was not much to behold at first, it greened up nicely and took on a life all its own.

Over the next couple of years, our little dogwood grew and grew. With a little pruning here and there, it shaped up to be one of our nicest trees on the property. After three years' time, that little stub we had given up on formed three strong branches from its original trunk. That year, the once-pitiful pauper of the flower bed stood proud, and for the first time since its transplant, was displaying some of the largest, most beautiful blooms we had ever seen. We could now sit on our very own porch swing, look to our right, and view one of the most spectacular dogwoods we had ever seen.

As I stood back and admired that wonderful little tree that came back to life, God impressed upon me what that tree really signified in our own story. Just like that little tree that survived a very rough transplant to enjoy a beautiful new life, Katrina and I have been able to build an amazing new marriage together. It has not been easy, especially in the early years of our stepfamily. What we have been through has not been for the faint of heart. Certainly, without God, it would not have been possible, as He provided a great deal of much-needed "pruning" along the way. Now, as our two little families grew into one big family of eleven (yes, that means *nine* children), our little stub of a tree, our existence that worldly statistics assumed would be hopeless, has grown strong branches.

The branch that has been the centerpiece of our growth is our strong marriage. Without it, we would have failed miserably. On each side of our marriage branch have grown two other branches. On one of those branches blooms our four older children, brought together by no doing of their own. Each of our fabulous four children are flourishing and have risen above our circumstances to become successes in their own right. Last is the third branch, the five beautiful children whom God has blessed Katrina and I with. They bring cohesion to our home and blossom each day as we excitedly watch them grow.

In John 10:10, the Lord Jesus said, "I have come that they may have life, and that they may have it more abundantly." Were it not for our branches growing from the firmly rooted trunk, none of this would have come to pass. When we thought life was hopeless, God provided us a hope, a future, and a new life. Also, in John 15:5, Jesus said, "I am the vine, you are the branches. He who abides in Me, and I in him, bears much fruit; for without Me you can do nothing."

Was everything perfect and tranquil in our house on the hill? Heavens, no! But at that time of our lives, when all of us needed a place to come together, we had settled in. We were home.

7

Another Kind of Itch

I suppose the worst place to get an itch, no matter the cause, is somewhere in the middle of your back where you can't quite reach it. I once had a boss who seemed to have that problem. On many occasions, when I would be in his office having a discussion, he would nonchalantly reach for a ruler or some other long object, lean over in his chair, and give his back a good scratch. Thankfully, he never asked me to do it! At other times, while he was standing just inside the doorway of my office visiting with me, he would attend to his infirmity by aligning the middle of his back with my door frame and rubbing his back in a side-to-side motion to ease what must have been a challenging skin problem. I have to say, during some of those sessions, while I was supposed to be listening to something important he had to say, visions of farm animals came to mind.

Having been around a farm for a good bit of my life has exposed me to cattle, goats, sheep, pigs, and other animals who do not hesitate to scratch themselves on whatever objects they can get their body up against. In recent years, the most hilarious of our farm animals have been the piglets, who will find a tree every moment they can and do a little happy dance up and down to satisfy their itches. (Now, I'm not saying my boss was a pig by any means, just making an observation here.)

Enough about managers, though. Let's put our focus on the subject of itching. Yes, I know what itching is about, for certain. As I've shared in a previous chapter, living in the South has its challenges as far as ticks, chiggers, mosquitoes, and other flying things are concerned, as well as all those pesky poison ivy leaves growing here and there whose oils cause explosive reactions on skin.

I remember when we were sodding grass on the side of our hill when we were getting our new yard established. As we rolled out pieces of sod, which turned our hill into a green, lush, grassy carpet, little did we know some stowaways had come along for the ride on the delivery truck. We figured it out soon enough, though. Apparently, with every pallet of sod that was delivered, chiggers and sand fleas tagged along as well. That caused us some irritation for a time afterward. If there is ever something in the environment that can cause a skin irritation, I'm likely to find it, and have since developed a healthy respect for the great outdoors, when and where to go, and what to do to prepare for and treat potential irritants. I'm not saying I'm a concrete-bound sissy who can never step foot in the great outdoors. What I am saying is that I have managed to collect a healthy dose of wisdom along life's way—a lot of it via the hard way, unfortunately.

A couple of years after moving into our house, I learned about another kind of itch, one that is not exactly a bodily itch, but more of a spiritual one. Once, while visiting with a group of friends in our Sunday School class at church, a husband began sharing about some interests he had had in pursuing another business venture, which would mean a total change in career direction. Without missing a beat, his experienced better half was happy to chime in and say something along the lines of, "Yeah, it's about that time again for him to get the itch to move onto something else."

I had never heard it put quite like that before. I was groomed early in life to satisfy that "itch" one time only by finding a career, latching onto it like a tick on a dog, and hanging on for life. Letting go was not an option my handlers had exposed me to. I was supposed to hang on tight, enjoy the ride to the top, and cruise into my sunset years with piles of cash and a pension.

That news came to me when I had been working the same job for the better part of fifteen years. Not exactly a long time, but I was, in essence, the tick. I had attached myself to the proverbial dog and was not budging. I had become somewhat comfortable, going to work in a familiar place with the same people, doing the same thing and feeling successful. I was happy with my cubicle, showing up at the same time, leaving at the same time, and getting a regular paycheck. At that point in my life, all I needed to do was sit back, relax, take my two percent raise every year, and live in my happy place. Don't get me wrong, I was working hard and doing a great job. But I was in a "line up, do what you're told, and everything will be wonderful" environment. I was deeply embedded in the corporate world. Perhaps a tick on a dog may not be the best analogy, but I was certainly getting quite comfortable inside the ear of a living and breathing organism.

For most of my life, I have had an aversion to risk. I generally haven't liked it in the least, and still don't for the most part. Security was my friend, and I perceived, like many folks do, that a well-established job at a reputable company for a long time meant security. As far as I was concerned, the riskiest thing I could do in the corporate world was to get out of my chair to walk away from my cubicle and go across the building to ask a person in another department a question. Risk did not include taking a job in another department, much less another company. Everything I knew and had carefully planned for depended on me riding smoothly in the boat, not rocking it. "Stay the course" was my motto. Doing so would create smooth sailing to the end until the first Social Security checks arrived, along with access to an overflowing 401(k) plan.

Katrina and I were by no means getting rich anytime soon. We were locked into our mortgage, had brought nine children into the world, and were doing our best to train them up in the way they should go while successfully paying the bills and saving a little. I suppose the higher mortgage had put a little more pressure on me to seek opportunities at work or otherwise get ahead, but I remained in my steady job for some time, happily seeking God's path for us and fulfilling our dream together in our established home. Life was good, and God had really blessed us beyond measure!

While our home life never had a dull moment and was full of adventures, I was maxed out in pay and lacked adventure at my current, long-term position at work. As a design drafter, I was literally going back to the drawing board day in and day out. I was good at what I did, but what had seemed like the most fulfilling and exciting job in the world a decade and a half earlier had become repetitive, something that lacked the excitement and newness that I had started longing for. Yes, I had the itch, the desire to move on to something else, something more.

Now, before you think I jumped on the crazy train, I wasn't even thinking of leaving the company. Oh, no! Remember me, the guy who hates risk? I wasn't ready for a move like that.

But do you know what I hate more than risk? I hate disobedience to our Lord. We had enjoyed the fruits of so many things at that point by listening to God that we never wanted to miss anything again, not ever.

It was about that time I began to explore a writing career. What started as a hobby morphed into something bigger, for a time at least. Given all the things that the Lord had taken us through and the excitement of our family life, I had a handful of people who had been encouraging me to start writing down some of the crazy stories I had been telling them. Not long afterward, I began sharing them with others in a blog.

During the same period, I became acquainted with a guy in our marketing department at work. One day, while walking past his office, I stopped to chat and saw him writing an article for a magazine. That grabbed my attention. Here was this guy, in the same building as me, getting paid to sit and write. Soon after that "chance" meeting, an opportunity came up to work for him, which would mean leaving my current position and taking a job in marketing. It all happened so fast, but it had been something Katrina and I had been praying about for quite a while. Before long, I moved from my comfy, established position in the design world to something totally out of my comfort zone and character, jumping into the world of marketing. Moving from the comfort I had grown to love, there was a steep learning curve that brought new kinds of stress I hadn't experienced in a while.

My sweet wife and I, along with others who had been praying for us, had no doubt God was in that career move. But it couldn't have come at a more inopportune time, at least from my perspective. I walked into that job at the height of the financial collapse of 2008 and 2009. Right after I started my new job, I watched what little I had in my 401(k) plan drop to rock bottom, along with our company's stock price. In addition to my job being a lateral move, which meant I received no pay increase for taking it, our company was having serious financial challenges along with the rest of the world. Nevertheless, we walked in faith and trusted God that He would continue to provide as I learned the ropes in my new position. That eventually paid off immensely, for which I am very grateful to God, my boss, and others who took me under their wings.

Before too long, my pay and benefits increased, and I was beginning to get my legs under me. Writing opportunities followed, and I eventually became a published author in several trade publications, boosting my confidence and fulfilling my dream of becoming published. But with success comes change. One thing that had changed with the job move was that I had begun traveling, something I'd never done much of before. For a while, it was exciting to get out and see other parts of the country, but my absence from home put new stresses on our family life and our marriage. But we soon settled into that new way of life, and since my travel rarely exceeded a half-dozen trips a year, we adjusted and made the best of it.

Not only had we adjusted to my new position at work, but we had settled in nicely to our home and family life. With my new career, faith in our God to provide, a beautiful family, and a wonderful dream home, what more could a guy ask for? We were blessed beyond measure!

8

Level Ground

Work and career had become my new focus, the journey I could give my all to, something new and exciting. I had an office with a window, and a real wooden door. I had advanced out of the cubicle world into the land of milk and honey, where I could look out the window of my own office and see ... well, the street outside where the cars passed by. Oh, and not to forget, I could look out in the other direction through the front glass of my tiny office and observe the expanse of cubicles as far as the eye could see. Best of all, I was no longer sitting in one of them. I had reached up, grabbed hold of the proverbial corporate ladder, and pulled myself up to what I perceived to be the next rung. I knew I needed to hang on tight, especially given my fear of heights. I never wanted to make it to the top, though: I understood that moving up in the organization meant change, something I did not like very much.

There was a lot to learn as my job transitioned from engineering to marketing. At the same time, Katrina had her hands full managing homeschooling challenges, mouths to feed, and a household to run—but she loved it. We were so glad we had made the decision for her to be a stay-at-home mom. We had to make sacrifices, watch our money closely, and most importantly, trust the Lord would do His part to guide us and provide for our needs. The blessings from Him were overwhelming, to say the least. God was so faithful!

When I had only been in my marketing position for a short time, God began stirring our hearts about moving our family somewhere else, but we weren't certain what that really meant. Moving didn't make much sense to us, especially since we were very settled at home and with my work. But a series of events that were unexplainable (other than by knowing that God was speaking to us directly) led us to seek the Lord about not only moving, but moving to *Italy*. Sounds completely crazy, huh? God was putting things about Italy in front of our faces from every direction, so many things that we couldn't deny for a moment it was Him speaking.

At that time in our lives, we were fighting an uphill battle regarding people's responses to our family size, and we were pretty beaten down. In the beginning, everyone had thought it was cool when we became a stepfamily like the Brady Bunch, but when people started comparing us to the Duggars, the giant family who reached stardom on their national TV show, it became unbearable.

It's funny how candidly people seem to think they can ask you questions or poke fun at you regarding your reproductive status, especially when you have nine children. Most people thought we were crazy, but we did have friends who were very supportive. I remember one friend whom I was close to at the time saying to me, "I really admire your faith to trust the Lord with your family. It's refreshing." That was a very timely encouragement to me, indeed!

After we prayed and sought the Lord diligently, we gave the idea of moving totally to Him, trusting Him to guide us. We surrendered our will to what God wanted. We were ready to follow Him to the ends of the earth if that's what it took to serve Him. We even went so far as to reach out to a gentleman in our church who had been intimately involved with missionary work. God put him in front of me one Sunday and I had an urge to talk to him, but I didn't follow through. A few days later, when looking through some things at work, his name came up completely at random. I knew immediately that I'd better follow through in obedience, which I did in short order. I shared my heart with him and he listened intently. We discussed some of our options regarding missionary work. After our discussion, he prayed with me and we continued to wait for further direction from the Lord. At the end of it all, in our pursuit of obedience, God shut that door and put it out of our minds. We were not moving to Italy, or even out of the country. But God had planted a seed in us that still needed further germination. We listened and waited, as the psalmist exhorts us:

Wait on the Lord;
Be of good courage,
And He shall strengthen your heart;
Wait, I say, on the Lord!
Psalm 27:14

Diapers were beginning to dwindle, along with the incessant crying. As Katrina was no longer with child or nursing an infant, which was a sad time for her, a new chapter of our life was beginning. All nine of our children were now walking on their own two feet. Our youngest was toddling along, while our four older children were moving toward careers at the end of their high school years. Most of our focus at home was on our youngest five children, with Katrina pouring herself into homeschooling, while I was off to the world of marketing every day working on my new career.

Up until that time, we had been attending the same church, the one our pastor had married us in over a decade earlier. We loved it there. We had several ministries we and the kids were involved in, but we were tired. We had worn ourselves out by going, going, going all the time. Having brought our four older kids through a plethora of activities with church, school, athletics, and otherwise, we had been asking the Lord what to do as our new generation of children were approaching the "busyness" years. Somehow, we just didn't see the value of keeping up the pace we had before, the pace our society seemed to demand of families. God gave us a clear answer. He reminded us we were the parents He had created to oversee the future of our precious children. We were responsible for setting the appropriate activity levels of our home. He clearly reminded us to stop caving to the pressure of society at large to do endless things that kept us busy, activities that added no real value to our home life or the future of our children.

Yes, God gave us wisdom, bringing us to a place of detachment and the decision to find a new church. Leaving the large congregation our kids had grown up in, which we had grown to love since our marriage began, was one of the hardest things we ever did. But God said it was time to go. We had to simplify our life and pursue a smaller, less busy church model, one that had fewer demands and fewer programs. We honestly didn't know what that could look like. But once God told us to go, He brought us to a community of believers in a smaller church setting, one that embraced a concept called family-integrated church. It was a simple church, and we were surrounded by families who pursued many of the same things we were pursuing, especially homeschooling.

A new time of growth came upon us. As our family was making new friends at our new, smaller church, we were gaining a new understanding of what church could look like. Little did we know this was only the beginning of our church and ministry journey. Katrina and I had been taught our whole lives to be in church every time the church doors were open, which had driven our schedules to a lot of religious activity. But we came to the realization that something was missing in the equation. It wasn't working, and it was not biblical, at least not the religious portion of it.

Hebrews 10:25 says, ". . . not forsaking the assembling of ourselves together, as is the manner of some, but exhorting one another, and so much the more as you see the Day approaching." It's funny. In all the years I have been a Christian and heard Hebrews 10:25 quoted, I don't remember the preacher ever backing up to quote Hebrews 10:24 along with it: "And let us consider one another in order to stir up love and good works." Those two verses, when quoted in order, make an amazing statement, which is exactly what Jesus would say—when we consider each other's needs, stirring up love and good works, we will naturally want to hang out together. We will love being together because we have grown to love one another. Sadly, much of the church in America has become what Jesus rebuked, a group of law-keepers pursuing religious activities. Don't get me wrong. I am not guilt-less, as I've pursued religious activities as much as anyone.

Our family became somewhat settled in our new church, which was headed in a good direction, and my job had become a mostly pleasant adventure. Then something happened that made life a little more interesting, an event that was somewhat miniscule in the whole scheme of things, at least at the time. But it was something I'd never experienced: my company was bought out by a much larger corporate conglomerate. One day, we were going to work as normal; the next day, we were being ushered into meeting rooms to explain that our company, one of the largest employers in our area and known for its local roots, had been gobbled up. Everything was presented to us by management as wonderful, and they promised everything would essentially remain the same. Things did stay the same, at least for a while.

In addition to writing and providing marketing material for our sales force and customers, my job included standing in front of people and doing product presentations. I didn't care for that at first, not in the least. There I was, standing in front of people, mostly delivering someone else's canned material, which was very difficult for me to do. I had stood in front of people teaching at church over the years, but that had become somewhat second nature, especially because I could speak from my heart and trust

God to guide me. But the public speaking at work was challenging. I knew that it would help develop me as a person, so I embraced it and began interjecting personal stories into what I was talking about. That helped me to connect with people like I never had before.

Proverbs 18:16 tells us, "A man's gift makes room for him, and brings him before great men." The talents God gives us, when we seek after them with all our hearts, will bring wealth to us. Essentially, when we use and grow the gifts God blesses us with, great men will seek after us for our talents.

At essentially the same time God was developing my career, I was asked to lead a portion of our church services, which again put me in front of our congregation every Sunday. Looking back, I can see the Lord polishing me, giving me confidence, boldness, and the courage to pursue His best desires for me.

I had become pretty good at what I was doing at work, gaining strength in my marketing legs. I had learned in the earlier part of my career that if you act with diligence and hard work and use the abilities God has gifted you with, success will follow. In past engineering roles, newcomers came along who couldn't understand how I could accumulate such a wealth of knowledge, but I had learned the fine art of repetition. When you do things the same way over and over for an extended period, it becomes second nature to you. It has been said this is how experts are born: it's not necessarily because of their innate ability to do things well, but because of their ability to polish and improve their skills until they can amaze others. But that can be troublesome for those who have difficulty staying the course or eventually get bored with what they are doing.

While I was doing well at work and home, something was still missing. I was going through the motions by pursuing excellence and getting a paycheck, one that was continually increasing. But that wasn't enough. Things in our life had sort of leveled off.

One big change that shook us immensely was the closure of our small church we had grown to love. At the end of that painful process, we found ourselves gathering in our living room with a handful of other former member families. This eventually became our home church fellowship. Just when we thought we had arrived on the flat ground of a plateau, where the view was amazing and we could camp out and settle in, things changed. God had something brewing in the kitchen that had a sweet aroma, but we hadn't quite determined what it was yet. Nonetheless, we were ready to pull ourselves up to His table and enjoy the feast of goodness He had been preparing for us, whatever that happened to be—which reminds me of a lunch I had a while back with a friend.

After doing some business together one day with my friend Sam, I wanted to take him to lunch at the place of his choosing. While a few spots would have topped my list of places to go that day, Asian food was not exactly one of them. My idea of Asian food is a buffet, where I can pick and choose what I want. Even when Katrina and I go to her favorite Vietnamese place, we just order the same fried rice and stir-fry we always get, with little hesitation. So many times, we have gone to a restaurant with the expectation of maybe trying something new, but in the end, we play it safe and order the same thing we have enjoyed for the past five years.

On that day with Sam, as we were approaching the Asian place, he was excitedly telling me about how it was one of his family's favorite places to go. He told me all about what he normally gets, and then proceeded to tell me about how his wife will just walk in there and tell the owner, "Just fix me whatever you like. Surprise me!" That sounded a bit off the charts for me.

Upon entering the fine establishment, I followed Sam over to the counter to place my order. Sam already knew what he wanted, which put the pressure on me to scan the extremely busy menu board and pick something without taking too long to choose. I nearly froze. In a split second, I made a choice—I could stand there for five minutes studying the board or go with the flow and order something quickly. I went with Sam's lead. Sam ordered and then when the owner looked at me expectantly, I said, "I'll have what he's having."

To many people, that probably did not sound like a risky venture, but to me, I had stepped into the unknown. On that occasion, hanging out with Sam was more important to me than my food choice. However, my risk paid dividends. In no time at all, Sam and I were both enjoying a wonderful bowl of noodles covered with several types of meat and drenched in a succulent sauce. The enjoyment and conversation that ensued far outweighed the risk of a bad meal choice.

I believe that is how most people really are in life. They play it safe, always go to the chain restaurant, and order the cheeseburger with fries. It's plain, predictable, and practical. Satisfying? Maybe, in a conservative, non-risky sort of way.

I am learning the art of adventure, developing the taste for a journey each day. While it's unlikely I will develop a taste for sushi anytime soon, I am continuing to explore options off the beaten path. Like the brave soul who considers every trip to a nice restaurant to be a culinary adventure, I am reaching the point in life where I am ready to sit down at God's table and say, "Surprise me!"

9

Making the Most of It

I f you are like me, you have probably seen all kinds of scenes
from Asian countries that show beautiful rolling hills, as far
as the eye can see, covered with garden terraces that make
the most of every inch of soil available. What you generally don't
see in abundance in those pictures are trees. The reason? For the
most part, crops don't grow very well under trees, especially trees
that provide a canopy of complete shade.

In our early days, while we were pondering a place to call
home, "living in the country" was a dream of ours that was
somewhat undefined. It could mean a farm with a barn and
cows roaming about or a wooded area with privacy and solitude.
Because our time and resources were limited in the beginning,
the place we decided to call home was ideal for us at the time.
It was our little acre of paradise where we were surrounded by
plentiful tall trees. I remember standing at the construction site
of our home, watching every move of the contractors to ensure

they did not cause any damage to the bark of a tree or push over any more trees than necessary. Because our house was built into the hill, the back door on the second floor came out to ground level on a deck my dad built. On either side of the deck, we were happy to have saved two giant oak trees that were within a foot or two of the edge of the back deck railing. It was really a wonderful blessing to have the tree coverage around most of the house. However, because we desired the trees for shade, growing grass and gardens on the ground we had available was quite a challenge.

We gave grass our best shot for a while after settling in. We had topsoil hauled in and spread out with no small effort, followed by a thorough coverage of Bermuda grass sod to hold the dirt on the hill. We were so proud of our grass that year. Our hill full of trees covered by a thick layer of grass looked like a planned golf course for a little while. The idea was to cover the hillside like a carpet, then seed it with shade grass in hopes of getting the grass to take root and spread. We worked on that for a time, but with every hard rain came more erosion of the grass seed and topsoil. It didn't do much for the yard on the hill, but it did a great job of starting grass in the ditch below, two hundred feet from our front door. Eventually, we let the yard revert to its original state, a forested leaf cover under a grove of oak and hickory trees. Not much mowing was required, but there were lots and lots of leaves to rake and burn as often as we cared to. I never remember a time when we did not have at least some portion of our one-acre yard covered in leaves.

Eventually, knowing we were determined to keep all that tree coverage, we gave up on grass entirely. Katrina was happy with shrubs and flower beds for a time, but one of the reasons we had wanted to settle in the country was to grow a garden. We wanted to have some of our own produce and teach the kids the value of hard work. We wanted them to know the joys of growing things in the garden, to expose them to the experiences we had lived through as we grew up. We did pursue growing a small garden, which I detailed in a blog post in 2010:

May 2010:

The stumps are aging and showing signs of relenting to the inevitable wear of the rain and sun that will bring them to their eventual rot. In time, they will become a part of the rich topsoil that our hill continues to produce year after year as the acorns and hickory nuts fall and the leaves decompose. A gentle mist has settled over us on this cool morning, a thick moisture after a strong storm moved through last evening.

The garden we have now, which did not exist a week ago, received a good drink from the storm, assuming it didn't wash away. There are not many flat areas for planting a garden on our little acre of heaven. Where our house sits and a few places near it are all that exist as far as horizontal ground is concerned. If a basketball were placed on the ground and released, chances are it would be several hundred feet away in seconds, destined for the road below. Although we installed a nice basketball goal next to our concrete driveway, playing requires a serious workout in rebounding to avoid lots of trips down the hill to retrieve the ball.

Our new garden came from Katrina's unrelenting determination and perseverance. When she gets something in her mind, she will stop at nothing to see it through. If I had a dollar for every time I've told her we don't have a place to plant a garden, I'd probably be able to buy her a piece of flat ground somewhere else to farm. Katrina doesn't take "no" for an answer.

Evidently, Katrina did not get her fill of gardening when she was a kid, but I sure did. I remember those hot summer days as we worked the garden, sitting around the wheelbarrow as we shelled peas and shucked corn. I reckon there's something to be said for teaching children God is the provider of the harvest, and I'm grateful our parents taught us just that. Most kids today think the corn or beans that come in a can from the store are made in some factory just like the rest of the prepackaged, processed foods we buy.

After years of telling me she wanted a garden, and after years of telling her we live on the side of a hill, Katrina finally threw my theory out the window and got busy anyway. On Saturday, armed with a hoe she had purchased a few days earlier, she began working on her garden on a small spot near our driveway. The spot was nothing but hard, red clay, piled there several years earlier during the house excavation.

Oblivious to what was going on, I began to wonder where Katrina had gone off to. I went outside looking for her, and to my surprise, there she was, scratching away at the ground like a squirrel on concrete. Now, I might not be the brightest crayon in the box, but I'm smart enough to know when Katrina is determined enough to ignore my advice and get to work, I'm better off just getting my tools and getting out there alongside her. She doesn't have to say another word to me. She just gets out there, gets busy, and sends out those inaudible signals that say, *We're planting a garden today, want to help?*

As I joined her, I realized right quick the shovel I was using was not going to cut it for breaking up this ground. I traded it for a pickaxe, and as I swung it relentlessly, breaking up the hard red clay, I envisioned my dad cruising along on his tractor breaking up the dirt with ease. Had it not been for the steepness of the terrain, I believe a clay pot manufacturer could have been located there years earlier.

It didn't take long before Katrina headed into the house to take care of the kids, leaving me with my underwhelming excitement to break the ground up properly. Some time later, she returned as I was bringing the pickaxe-swinging to a close, having completed my aerobic workout for the day. I left her to rake the clods of earth out evenly and moved several yards away into the woods to begin excavating for topsoil. As she raked, I delivered several wheelbarrow loads of fresh topsoil from the woods, thus completing my gardening for the day. The garden plot was now in the competent hands of my lovely wife, the green thumb of our family.

As Katrina continued spreading the dark soil for the garden and readying the rows for seeds, I moved on to something else entirely. I took our leaf rake and began cleaning off our trail in the woods. We had been using the same path for some time now, but it had become leaf-covered again after the passing of fall and winter. We all loved walking in the woods, but hated the idea of it being too overgrown, so I began clearing it once again.

The kids soon discovered what I was doing, and as they followed our clean trail I was creating in the woods, they abandoned Mommy the gardener, who was still working feverishly at the trailhead garden spot. The farther the kids and I went into the woods, the more they seemed to forget about the gardening and become more excited about the trail. I reminded them a couple of times that they should go back and see how the garden was coming along, but they followed me nonetheless.

Soon, Mommy's familiar voice yelled, "It's ready!" The kids dropped me like a hot potato to go and plant their seeds, which they had selected earlier in the week when they were at the store hoe shopping. I was left to fend off the winding vines of poison ivy in the forest as they headed back to the vegetable garden. As I brought my trail work to a close, the team of gardeners completed their labor as well. They came down the trail to have a look at my work, and we all emerged from the woods to have a look at their rows of potential produce. Finished at last!

I don't suppose this garden will deliver a bumper crop of anything that will save us very many trips to the store, but the kids will always remember their experience of watching those tiny seeds they planted in the earth come alive. Who knows? Before it's all said and done, we may just abandon our house on the hill and our postage stamp garden and settle into somewhere that's flat and fertile. But, until then, this will be home sweet home for us.

Was the last sentence of that narrative some sort of premonition? Was something inside me urging me toward the idea that we may, in fact, move on from our paradise on the hill to somewhere else at some point? Perhaps it was. But how could that be? We had built our dream home, the place we planned to be for the rest of our lives, the place to watch our kids grow up. Wedding celebrations would be had there, along with priceless memories of holiday gatherings galore.

Maybe it was just the gardening that would have to go, given the fact that despite all our wonderful woods, we lived only five minutes away from a grocery store in either direction, where vegetables were sold in convenient abundance.

10

Chasing Jaguars

When I was a young boy growing up in the great state of Arkansas, we were exposed to all manner of country life, for which I am forever grateful. One of the things that has been grafted onto our family tree was a love for hound dogs, especially beagles. I'm not exactly sure how it came about, but for whatever reason, my dad introduced several beagles into the family over the years. He loved having them around. And one of the primary things that beagles love to do—what God put them on this earth to do—is to hunt.

In those early beagle years, I was thrilled to have a wonderful, friendly dog at our place to lie on the front porch and just have around. When we ventured out on our property, away from their comfortable spot on the porch, I learned how much they loved to chase rabbits. So, we began to take the dogs with us, along with our guns, to chase rabbits out of some thicket in hopes of shooting some and bringing them home to throw into a pot of stew. While it was a wonderful thing to bring home some wild game for food, my dad, the beagles, and I loved the hunt most of all.

On our hunting expeditions, the beagles would be drawn to an area thought to be the hiding place of a rabbit. They would put their noses to the ground and get busy doing what they did best. After a quick evaluation of the area, the beagles would start yelping, excited to have found the scent of a varmint, hopefully a rabbit. The chase would be on as the hounds continued to sniff, search, and yelp. We attempted to keep up with them down the first rabbit trail, but before long, they would turn and head into another direction, then another, and another. At times, the hunt would be fruitful, but at other times, it would wind up taking us in circles, no rabbit in sight.

Stick with me, here. I am about to take you down a rabbit trail or two, but if you persist, we will get to the pot of stew at the end.

Yes, beagles love rabbits; their nature is predictable in that way. But what are some of the things that we as people love and cling to, like beagles love their rabbit hunting? What is that one thing so important to you that if someone snatched it away, the true *you* would come out, perhaps shamefully? Is it security, a trinket, your bank account, your 401(k) plan, a stuffed animal you had as a kid, the car you drive, a photo in your wallet, a family heirloom? What is it exactly? It may be multiple things.

For me, it was control. I love to be in control. I suppose many folks do. I'm not talking about being a controlling person, one of those control freaks who loves to manipulate other people.

As best I can tell, I don't fit that profile. To me, control simply means having a plan, knowing where I'm going, eliminating all possible risks so the plan can move forward. Who wouldn't want that, right? When plans get interrupted, modified, or canceled, I don't like it in the least. But I'm learning to roll with change.

Another form of control is planning for tomorrow, the next day, the next month, the next year, and even a lifetime. Planning for the future is good stewardship, which God prescribes for us in Scripture. It even says in the book of Proverbs that a man should get his fields established before building his household. That makes amazing sense to me.

Because planning was my strength and I wanted to steer the ship, Katrina and I decided I would be in charge of the budget and planning for the future at our home. When we first married, things were very tight financially. We didn't have much, but we were getting by for the most part. Although I was the primary breadwinner, Katrina also worked outside the home as a preschool teacher. It was work that was rewarding to her, and it helped to make ends meet. However, in the first summer we were married, we were going to have all four of our kids at home all summer, which meant they would have to attend the preschool Katrina worked at—and it wasn't going to be for free.

Well, after much prayer, pencil pushing, and budgeting for those few months, we had two options: We could keep the kids with her all day at the preschool, which didn't make sense financially (and wouldn't be best for the kids). Or she could quit her work, which also did not make sense financially. However, after seeking the Lord, we knew He was calling her to turn in her resignation. Although we would suffer a financial loss for a time, we valued her being able to stay at home with the kids: it paid dividends money couldn't buy.

We never looked back, and through all their growing-up years, Katrina remained the stay-at-home mom she had always longed to be. God blessed us for that decision to choose what was right for the children over our bills and bank account. For a guy who wanted to control every penny going in and out of our budget, God taught me a valuable lesson. He can provide and stretch things in ways we can't put a pencil to. That was our marriage's first lesson in trusting in the Lord's provision.

Because we already had four children when we married, having children together was not exactly on the forefront of our minds. We felt like we were overloaded beyond measure trying to figure out the ins and outs of being a stepfamily. There were joyful noises mixed with weeping and gnashing of teeth. It was not for the weak at heart, believe me. As much as we tried to convince everyone we were a blended family, I think the only evidence of blending was that we felt like we had been through a blender. Something was missing in our family. It wasn't too long before Katrina and I began praying fervently to determine if God desired us to bring children of our own into our new family. We thought we had that area of our life figured out, too, but God had other plans.

During all the years of driving to work, I was diligent at listening to encouraging things on Christian radio, whether it was music or talk shows, much the same as today's podcasts. In early May 2000, I was driving to work listening to a show called *Focus on the Family*, which I had been accustomed to doing for years. That day, they aired a broadcast discussing a book called *The*

Prayer of Jabez. I had never heard of the author or the book, but I listened intently as I drove along. They had chosen the topic of prayer because the day I was listening fell on the National Day of Prayer. After their discussion, the hosts compelled Christians to gather at their local churches during the lunch hour to pray for the country and other needs.

I knew our church was going to be open, but it was too far from my work for me to go there on my lunch hour. When I arrived at work, I started fumbling through the phonebook, looking for a church nearby where I could pray during lunch. I stumbled onto a church I had learned of from several friends: Haven Heights Baptist Church. Since it was nearby, I went there during my lunch break.

There was nobody there in the church sanctuary that day, so I pretty much had the place to myself. I had a good time of prayer, and even prayed the Prayer of Jabez, which says: "Oh, that You would bless me indeed, and enlarge my territory, that Your hand would be with me, and that You would keep me from evil, that I may not cause pain!" (1 Chronicles 4:10)

I was thinking, *Hey, that would be pretty good for God to increase my territory financially.* That was my flesh thinking, always fixating on money and possessions. God had a different plan, though. I finished up my praying, went back to work, and headed home for the evening.

The next day, there I was, driving to work, listening to the second half of the message from the day before about *The Prayer of Jabez.* It was becoming apparent to me that God was trying to tell me *something,* but I had no idea what it was at that point. After hearing the message, I went to work and just couldn't get the radio show off my mind. I had prayed to God before for His help and guidance about various things but had not really prayed and asked God to specifically bless me and expand my borders. This was new territory for me. I pondered that message all morning, letting it soak in while I worked; it was eating at my soul. So, I decided to drive back over to the church at lunch and pray.

I came to the church, and again had the place to myself. It seemed strange to be in that large sanctuary praying all alone, but I proceeded. Just like the day before, I began praying and then opened my Bible to the Prayer of Jabez. I've never been one to use a prewritten prayer, but I recited it again, asking for God's blessing and for Him to enlarge my territory.

Wow!

I had no idea what those words meant for me until that very moment. Suddenly, I could feel the presence of God like someone was sitting right next to me. *He was there!* As I wept uncontrollably, He spoke to me in a still, small voice and gave me the peace Katrina and I had been seeking for months.

As I said before, we had been praying fervently that God would reveal Himself to us about whether we should have any more children. Yes, it seemed easy for Katrina to pursue that direction based on her emotions, baby smells, and the ticking of her biological clock. But every time we had talked about it, she would ask me, "Well, has God given you an answer yet?" She was trusting me to be the spiritual leader of our home God ordained me to be, to make the decision, to go before God Almighty, and to come back with an answer.

When God was there with me, He took away all the doubts I had been clinging to. I had been worried about money, how it would affect us and our other children, and the fact that there was no way (in our minds) we could live in our current house with any more family members. But God gave me a peace about all of that and let me know it was all in His hands.

I stood up that day in that quiet, seemingly empty church, having been in the presence of God. He confirmed for me that He was going to provide for us, and that I should let go of that burden and let Him carry it for us. I did. The rest is history.

A Few Years Down the Road

Loving material things can be detrimental to a person's physical, mental, and spiritual condition. I have had to learn that the hard way. There are some folks in religious circles who believe that if you think positive thoughts enough, or just ask God for what you want, you will get what you ask for. However, there is a fine line between asking God to bless you with things for your own selfish desires and asking for things that you really need. I'm going to go down another rabbit trail and tell you an interesting story, one that took me in a direction that really grabbed my attention.

Now, I like a fine automobile as much as the next guy, but there is a difference between appreciating a fine car versus being in love with one. I was fortunate enough to have my dad guiding me as we built an amazing hot rod truck when I was in high school, from the inside out. We were both proud of that truck and the work we had done, but I can't say I loved it. Loving things is a dangerous proposition. If you have ever been in one of those high-pitched sales presentations, particularly those that encourage you to join some multilevel-marketing organization, you may have been exposed to someone saying something like, "If you could have whatever you want, what would it be?" Generally, anyone with a pulse shifts their mind into overdrive, thinking of the bills they would like to have paid off, a nice house, travel, a nice car, or whatever other luxuries come to mind.

Remember that three-story house I dreamed about when I was a boy? With God's help, we built it. When I was in high school and college, I dreamed of having a good job with an established company. God blessed me with that as well. God had also blessed me with a beautiful wife and thriving family. What more could a guy possibly need, right?

In our early years, Katrina and I took pride in learning to save up to buy vehicles for cash. It wasn't easy, but we were sick of multiple car payments and liked the idea of never having another one. We had been saving up for a car for quite some time, and praise the Lord, with good money management, we were getting close to being able to replace my worn-out 1998 Honda Civic. I was shelling out more on maintenance than I desired, and it seemed to be a great time to invest the money in a newer used car instead.

Then for reasons I can't explain, something grabbed my attention. I'm not sure if I saw one in a TV show, movie, or what, but I latched onto the idea of owning a Jaguar. Why that car, you ask? Your guess is as good as mine. The perception in our rural part of the world is that most real men drive a four-by-four pickup, not a snooty European car. Nonetheless, I had the fever. I even went so far as to order a sales brochure from the nearest dealer, which was hours away from us. I still stumble upon that old brochure from time to time in stacks of memorabilia. May it be a reminder to me, every time I stumble upon it, of a thorn I never want to have in my flesh again.

Since we had become very keen on the concept of praying for blessings from God, thanks to that little-known guy
in the Bible named Jabez, it seemed to make sense to ask
God to bless us with the car I wanted—I mean *needed*. And
if you're going to dream, why not dream big, right? I can't
quite remember how those prayers went, how I was asking
God to bless us with that car. As a family man with a wife
and nine children, I should have been praying for a small bus,
but we were already driving something in that category. What
I needed was a great commuter car, one that required nearly
zero maintenance and was good at the gas pump. Not sure
how a Jaguar fit into those categories, but I had convinced
myself it would check all the boxes.

Another blessing that came with our house on the hill was a
pleasant, predictable commute to work, about twenty minutes
one way. After a while coming and going at the same times, you
tend to see a lot of the same vehicles along the way, so when
something out of the ordinary passes by, it catches your eye. One
day, on my way to work, I saw it, just up ahead. There it was: a
Jaguar, the same model I had been foaming at the mouth for.
Wow! That was just too cool, especially since I rarely saw a car
like that in our part of the world.

A few days after the first Jaguar sighting, I was on my way
home from work and stopped to get gas. There I was, pump-
ing gas and thinking about nothing special except getting home,
when suddenly, there it came—the Jaguar! Then the most incred-
ible thing happened as I walked around the back of my car. The
personalized license plate on the Jaguar had the name JABEZ on
it. There was no way this was happening!

Moments later, an ordinary-looking guy stepped out of the gas station and walked over to his car, the Jaguar. Now, I don't normally strike up conversations with strangers, but I had to ask him about the license plate and the car.

"It's a long story," he replied, "but I asked God for this car, and He gave it to me." We were both wanting to be on our way, but I couldn't let him go without asking for his name and number, as I wanted to hear the rest of his amazing story. I later called him up and made lunch plans for the following week.

Time stood still for the next several days as I anticipated our meeting. My prayers must have increased in fervency as I thought about that Jaguar that God had given the guy as a gift. Then just at the last minute, Mr. Jabez (not his real name) called and said he had to cancel our lunch due to a family emergency, and maybe we could schedule it for another time. For some reason, after all my built-up anticipation for our meeting, it never happened. We tried to connect later, but life has a way of moving on, and I never was able to hear his amazing story about God's blessing. In fact, I never saw him or his car again.

Shortly after my chance meeting with Jaguar Guy Number One, I was introduced to Jaguar Guy Number Two: Mr. Dan Miller, a career expert and author of the book *48 Days to the Work You Love*. Dan's book had been instrumental in guiding me along the way with work, and he regularly sent emails to his subscribers. Not long after the Jaguar sightings, Dan sent out an email that talked about the latest car he was going to have to let go of. He had been a car collector for many years, and had really enjoyed the one he'd been driving, but he was upgrading to something else. He offered his Jaguar at what seemed like a somewhat reasonable price (along with the chance to personally meet him at his home), but it was an older, different model than I was looking for. At first glance, it seemed like I could not pass it up, like it was divine guidance from Heaven above. But I had no peace about it at all. In the end, I did pass it up.

Divine guidance did, in fact, get my attention. God grabbed me by the scruff of the neck and shook me back to reality, bringing me out of my stupor. After much prayer and time with God, I determined it was time to abandon my nonsensical pursuit of a Jaguar. It didn't make good sense financially, it would have created the debt we were trying to avoid, and it was not practical for what we needed. Most of all, I didn't like the way it was making me think, feel, and act. I knew God wasn't exactly pleased with me during the process, either. Would it have been acceptable to own that nice car? Perhaps, under different circumstances. But I think it would have owned me instead.

I grumbled as I continued to drive my old Honda Civic for quite a while longer, which had its moments. We were not destitute, but we had chosen to forego replacing the failed air conditioner and save the money instead for our future car purchase. We later had some friends, Jimmy and Vanessa, who had heard about our lack of air conditioning in the worst part of the hot summer. Jimmy told me God had impressed upon him to pay to have our air conditioner repaired. He said God had blessed his business immensely, and now God wanted him to bless others. Wow, what a generous gift! I protested to him at first, telling him it was not necessary and we could really afford it but had chosen to save the money instead. He was quick to remind me that it would rob him of a blessing if I didn't allow him to repair our car. So, we proceeded with having the air-conditioner repaired, which blessed us all beyond measure. God got my attention, and I turned my grumbling about my old car into thanksgiving. Had I sold my old car and pursued the Jaguar I didn't really need, I would have missed that amazing opportunity to be blessed in a way that was totally unexpected. That's how God works. Oh, how he loves to bless His children with good gifts:

> *Ask, and it will be given to you; seek, and you will find; knock, and it will be opened to you. For everyone who asks receives, and he who seeks finds, and to him who knocks it will be opened. Or what man is there among you who, if his son asks for bread, will he give him a stone?*
> *Or if he asks for a fish, will he give him a serpent? If you then, being evil, know how to give good gifts to your children, how much more will your Father who is in heaven give good things to those who ask Him!*
> Matthew 7:7-11

The House for a Lifetime

As I have unpacked and revealed some of the human condition (especially mine!), the fact is that so many of us want to be in total control of our environment, to be our own god and call all the shots. That can get in the way of us trusting the real God, the one and only true God, for our needs. There's nothing wrong with possessing nice things: people have owned things for thousands of years. But nice things have also owned people for thousands of years, and it will be that way until the end of time.

A couple of passages come to mind that help solidify where I'm going here:

Give me neither poverty nor riches—feed me with the food
allotted to me; lest I be full and deny You, and say,
"Who is the Lord?" or lest I be poor and steal,
and profane the name of my God.
Proverbs 30:8-9

Now godliness with contentment is great gain.
For we brought nothing into this world, and it is certain
we can carry nothing out. And having food and
clothing, with these we shall be content.
1 Timothy 6:6-8

When we designed our house on the hill, we dreamed of things we wanted in a home, things that would bring value, features that would improve our lives and make our home an enjoyable place to live for our children and grandchildren. We literally saw it as the place where we would build up our family and put down deep roots for the rest of our lives. The house represented the fact that we had rebuilt our lives together and were thriving in our new marriage and family. It would open opportunities for our children, including those yet to be born, as we trusted God for increase. We only had a glimpse of how much that house was going to bless us, to help us get through the season we were entering.

We loved that house. The love we had for it was not borne from a possessive "I must have this!" outlook. For many years, we had been collecting puzzle pieces here and there until we had the time and resources to put the giant puzzle together. It wasn't like we went to the store and picked out a thousand-piece, off-the-shelf jigsaw puzzle of someone else's house. This was the custom version, the one we had picked up clues about for what seemed like forever. Then it really happened: it was built.

In the beginning stages of the house, probably right after we had it in the dry, I was making what seemed like daily trips to the various hardware stores and home centers, collecting one thing after another from a never-ending list. Somehow, in those early days of the process, before we were stressed near the end when most of the budgeted money was gone, I determined to buy the nice wooden porch swing we had always wanted. While it may have been only a little over a hundred bucks or so, it was one of those things we did not want to overlook. We wanted to make sure we had our swing before the first mortgage payment came. Looking back at all the years of rocking in that swing together, it turned out to be a wise decision—amazing memories were made in that swing.

What were some of the other amenities we were looking for in a house? Well, of course that swing needed a full wraparound porch on the front that gave us a view of the woods in three directions. A fireplace was a must, along with three levels and two staircases, six oversized bedrooms (all with walk-in closets), a full bathroom on every floor, and an oversized master bathroom complete with hot tub, walk-in shower, double sinks, and a picture window for viewing the woods outside and the stars at night. The large kitchen, dining room, and living room, all on the entry floor, were a must for enjoying the company of our friends and family.

Because Katrina was such an amazing teacher and home-maker, a schoolroom with a supply closet was downstairs just off the living room, as well as a large laundry room (complete with laundry chute) and pantry next to the kitchen. Oh, and who could forget we made the garage extra wide and deep to ensure our two vehicles could easily park indoors without any chances of door dings? Walk-in access to multiple attic storage areas was required for all the things we would want to accumulate for the rest of our lives. After all, we were a growing family. Some of the coolest rooms in the house, though, were the little nooks under the staircases. Those rooms were just the right size for all the little people to camp out and make cozy spots for playing, reading, or hiding.

Oh, we used that house with all our might! Because we had no real yard at first, the full-length porch became the place to ride bikes and scooters and to skate as fast as we could. On one end of the porch, we fit one of the best investments we'd ever bought: a very rigid and durable plastic kiddie pool. Katrina managed to take one of our extra playground slides and wedge it between the porch rail and pool, which made for an amazing water slide. The kids would go catch water turtles from the nearby creek and let them swim in the pool with them. On our first Christmas in the house, the kids received a trampoline from their grandpar-ents we were crazy enough to assemble and leave up in the living room, of all places. The trampoline moved outside as the weather improved, but the next year the kids were gifted a jungle gym, which of course stayed in the living room for a time.

Now that our kids are nearly grown and have begun con-
fessing their sins, we've learned that some of their best memories
were getting on pillows and sliding down the solid oak staircase
into the front door. At other times, while we were away and they
were staying at home with their older siblings, they would pile all
the laundry in a giant heap and jump down the laundry chute.
Yes, our children seemed to have lived in one giant play place.
Oh, and who could forget that the kids and our dog Sammy
loved climbing up on the roof, which was easily accessible from
the backyard? It's a wonder they all survived to tell about it!

Then there was the hundred-acre wood. The expanse of property that bordered our home was an endless *outdoor* playground.
Our family had many memorable places we loved to go, including
Tree Rock, The Mud, The Mountain, The City Trail, Snake Rock,
and The Creek. The possibilities were endless for adventures!

We really loved our home. We had poured ourselves into that
place like nothing else we had ever done in life. Our family was
expanding and our children were growing up there, with all the
room for growth and adventure they ever needed. It really was hard
to imagine that we had come to that place, a dream come true.

Then one day, God impressed me to let it all go. This had
come up before, when we had considered moving to Italy, and
again when we were struggling with gardening space. But this
time was different. The weight of it all was bearing down on
me with an indescribable heaviness. I couldn't shake it. However,
when I shared that premonition with Katrina, I soon discovered
I was one lonely lunatic. The word from the Lord hadn't reached
her ears yet. She thought it was ridiculous, that I must have been
hearing things and losing my mind. So, we waited and prayed for

a time, to ensure what I was hearing was right. I had no doubts, but I wanted to bring Katrina along in her time, to make sure we were both confident that God was telling us the same thing.

More time passed, and the focus seemed to not only include the house, but the many things we had been accumulating over the years in that place. I had built a workshop out back that was now full of various useful things. I had also built a giant playhouse for the kids, one that included a dormer on the front with a heart-shaped window, flower boxes under the front windows, and a second level with a handmade ladder that went into the inside loft. We loved our existence on that hill so very much, getting settled into home more and more as each year passed.

Then a little messenger came along. When kids deliver a message from God, it usually doesn't come with a loud, thundering voice from the heavens, and it's usually when you least expect it. One day, in July 2013, little Olivia and I were swinging in the porch swing. We were just having a big time together, talking, singing, and swinging. But suddenly, Olivia grew serious, turned to look at me, and, with her sweet five-year-old voice, said, "This is not our home."

I said, "Really?"

She said, "Yeah, Heaven is our home, not here."

I was amazed and speechless. As we went back to swinging, Olivia had no clue how valuable her words had been, but I sensed deep in my soul things were about to change for us in a dramatic fashion.

God eventually brought Katrina to the same place I had been for a time, and we began taking steps to grab hold of the vision God had given us and move away. In many ways, it didn't make sense in the least. We wondered why God would help us build such a wonderful place to live, only to tell us to let it all go. But God's ways are not our ways. Despite our sadness and bewilderment, we embraced being obedient to our Lord. That meant we had lots to do in the days, weeks, and months ahead.

In this chapter, I discussed a few proverbial rabbit trails centered around one theme—worldly distractions. What are the distractions keeping us from serving God and embracing His ultimate plan for us? I wanted to retain control of my family size, my bank account size, the car I had in the driveway, and essentially everything else I was consumed with. My family and most other people I know are not that much different.

It is a lifelong struggle to maintain some semblance of peacefulness when, all along, peace and tranquility come from the Father above. He is our Source of lifelong peace. Like all the times we long to go back to our earthly homes when we are away on trips, we must realize we are in a continuous state of sojourning here on Earth. We are longing for our heavenly home, the one God has prepared for those who love Him.

11

Everything Has a Shelf Life

I am old, but I was once young.

Hmm, let me rephrase that. I have been around a while. Not long enough, mind you, but long enough to have seen a few things, gathered some perspective, and gained a bit of wisdom along the way. Let's just say I'm still in the "young" category, without a hill to pass over just yet. I'm not interested in being over the hill anyway, as I still have a mountain or two left to scale, Lord willing.

Am I deteriorating? Yes, I suppose so. I'm feeling pretty good about my general health, but if I could see the inner workings of this tent I'm dwelling in, there are probably several inefficiencies I'm unaware of. I have a slight twinge in my knee, a throbbing in my hand, and a pesky pain in my wrist that hasn't left me yet. The mind seems clear mostly, but that depends on the time of day and how much black coffee I've consumed as the day goes on. I used to think I could drink coffee from sunup to sundown and still sleep like a baby, but I'm beginning to see that my eyes do not shut as tightly as they used to, that getting into a restful place at night is not as easy as it used to be. I used to wonder why some older folks were that way, having difficulty getting to sleep and staying asleep. I am beginning to learn what that is all about, unfortunately.

According to the Second Law of Thermodynamics, when things are left alone, they will deteriorate over time. Essentially, unless things are improved upon, they tend to get worse over time. Let's take houses, for instance. When a new house is built, the proud homeowner waltzes in, proud as a peacock, puts up a mailbox, buys the new lawnmower they've always desired, and expects to live happily ever after. Surely, everything at their new abode is going to operate perfectly forever and ever. However, time and the nature of things have a way of creeping up on a person just when they least expect it, especially when their bank account can ill afford to handle a home repair on the indestructible dwelling they thought they had purchased a few years earlier. Sometimes there are events that accelerate the entire process, such as an unforeseen accident, a natural disaster, or the invasion of termites or ants that desire to live alongside you.

Let me tell you about one such event that took place at our brand-new home, the place that we thought would last forever, something I wrote about in some of my early writings:

February 17, 2008:

Early morning times are my favorite. I appreciate that time of day because most others don't have the same appreciation. That means I get to enjoy some peace and quiet while so many others are doing the same with their face smashed into a pillow, mouth wide open with dreamtime drool accumulating in a puddle.

One Sunday morning, I was sitting on the loveseat in the living room. The house was quiet, but time would soon bring that to an end. No sun was shining in the windows to wake anyone up since it was a cloudy, rainy day out. But soon the children would arise and explode onto the scene, anxious to create or experience something spectacular.

I had been up for a while, having had some quiet time with the Lord, as well as reading and writing a little in my journal. I stood up for a moment to go to the bathroom to make room for more coffee. While in the bathroom washing my hands, I began to ponder the sink and the ignorant decision we made in purchasing it.

The sink, cabinet, and mirror combination had been a real bargain. We had thought it had been such a bargain that we bought two of them, one for the downstairs bathroom and one for the third-floor bathroom.

Given our inexperience with sinks, although we'd been using them our entire lives, we hadn't noticed anything out of the ordinary with them until after we had lived in our house for a while. You see, a good bit of our family time was spent in the downstairs portion of our dwelling, the center stage of our three-ring circus. Many times, during any given day, Katrina could be found doing laundry, dishes, meal preparation, or all manner of other things, all while doing her best to keep a close watch over the kids. At that juncture in life, most of the smaller children loved playing in the sink in the downstairs bathroom. For some reason they were drawn to it. They would either stand on the toilet or drag up the little stool, fill the sink with water, and play to their hearts' content. No problem, right?

One of the kids, who shall remain nameless (because I have forgotten who it was), had a real problem with not turning the water off after washing their hands. The main problem with that was that they would leave the stopper in the bottom of the sink. Normally, that wouldn't be that big a deal, but that sink, the one we thought was such a "deal," had no overflow drain hole in the back of it.

One day, we learned just how valuable overflow drains are.

Katrina, being the outstanding busy mother she is, was not far away in the laundry room, folding some clothes while the kids played. She has always been good at directing the children to find things to do while she's busy, so she wasn't worried about them at the moment. She soon came out of the laundry room, walked across the kitchen floor, into the living room, and into *squish, squish, squish* …

Water! *Ah*! It was everywhere! And guess what: the sink was still running, with no child in sight!

Katrina quickly went to work. She turned off the water, grabbed all the towels she could, and went to retrieve the Shop-Vac, which we were thankful to have on hand. She spent a long time sopping up and sucking up water, and upon the completion of that task, she put a fan on the floor to dry the remaining moisture. Pooling or spilled water mixed with wood, carpet pad, carpet, or other building materials do not contribute well to the longevity of a home. Thankfully, she did an amazing job at containing the mess and averting further catastrophe.

As I stood at the sink for a moment, shaking my head side to side to snap out of that flashback, I moved on and made my way to the kitchen to retrieve my second cup of coffee. I soon settled back down to enjoy the last few quiet moments of the morning, happy that nothing unsettling was going on ... at least, nothing I knew of yet.

That story is a prime example of how quickly things can change. Left alone, the house could have had significant damage, including wood rot or mold. In the house where we now live, which was built around the same time as our previous house on the hill, we have had a few things creep up that required the immediate attention of a professional. One such event involved a chicken leg.

My queen and I have the privilege of having our master suite in the downstairs portion of our current dwelling. This room in the heart of our home is easily accessible without stairs, praise the Lord! In fact, when we were looking for this home, stairs were crossed off the list of desired features. The downside of our bedroom being on the bottom floor is that it is right below some of the activity that goes on upstairs, namely our boys' room and the bathroom. On any given night, as we are attempting to slumber, we can hear every step, every motion, and every trickle of water flowing in the bathroom. Not extremely noticeable, mind you, but it's there nonetheless, especially when we want the house to be silent.

One of my habits, which I am working to improve on, is drinking coffee up into the evening, sometimes even right before bed. Inevitably, what goes in must come out, sometimes sooner than later. On one such night, after I had made my bleary-eyed trek to and from the master bathroom, I paused in the middle of the bedroom, thinking I had just felt a drop of water on my face. I went back to bed and brushed it off as temporary insanity, but before long I heard a distinct sound, something that had a different rhythm from the shower one of our boys was taking upstairs at that ridiculous hour of the night. Listening intently, I stood up and walked to the end of the bed. Sure enough, not only could I reach out and feel a *drip, drip, drip* in my hand, but I could also feel a puddle forming in the carpet. Some towels and a bowl helped me put off the issue until I could deal with it after the sun came up the next morning.

Upon further investigation, we determined a plumber would be needed to repair a pipe in the wall that was connected to the upstairs shower. By then, some discoloration had already occurred on the sheetrock of our white ceiling. We drained the water out of the ceiling, but the water had created an odd pattern, which I noticed the most, given the fact it was nearest to my side of the bed. That was one of those times I was thankful for my lovely bride's poor eyesight. With her glasses or contacts, she can see normally, but when she comes to bed, she can't see well at all.

After the plumber dealt the blow to our budget and fixed the problem upstairs, we had to fix the discoloration of the sheetrock. Now, I am a man. Most men can tolerate things not looking quite right, especially regarding the aesthetics of a home's interior. In my opinion, the bedroom ceiling could wait. Who would notice, right? This was our private space where hardly anyone ever came. Some time passed after the water incident, and I wondered why Katrina had not insisted on getting the primer, paint, and a roller out to fix the unsightly spot on the ceiling. Then one night, as we were lying in bed about to shut off the lights, I made the mistake of opening my mouth and allowing my vocal cords to operate without the use of my brain.

I turned over to Katrina and said, "Have you noticed that the spot on the ceiling looks just like a chicken leg?"

"I can't see anything," she said. "I already took my contacts out."

Then, reaching for her glasses and leaning over to my side of the bed, she had a good look at what I'd been seeing for weeks. She agreed: it really resembled the shape of a drumstick! We primed and painted the ceiling soon after that.

As indestructible and well-built as some things seem, including a home, everything has a shelf life. Nothing lasts forever, at least not on this earth. Jesus told us this as He spoke to the people during His ministry:

> *Do not lay up for yourselves treasures on earth,*
> *where moth and rust destroy and*
> *where thieves break in and steal;*
> *but lay up for yourselves treasures in heaven,*
> *where neither moth nor rust destroys*
> *and where thieves do not break in and steal.*
> *For where your treasure is, there your heart will be also.*
> Matthew 6:19-21

It's all going to burn. All the stuff people accumulate on this earth will one day be destroyed, gone forever. I can leave my house from any direction and within a mile or two, show you houses that have fallen in or been destroyed by the natural occurrence of time, weather, and deterioration. Even the house I now live in, not even twenty years old, continues to slowly decline into a lesser state of existence with every passing day. As Paul reminds us, "We brought nothing into this world, and it is certain we can carry nothing out" (1 Timothy 6:7).

This place, this planet, is a sinking ship. Do not waste another day heaping up things that will not last. Invest in the lives of others to ensure that when we reach our heavenly home, we will see all those whose lives we have touched. Oh, may we be found worthy to have been a positive influence on those around us, a light to them in such a way as to see them when we get there. Reminds me of the chorus of another hymn, "When We All Get to Heaven":

> *When we all get to heaven,*
> *What a day of rejoicing that will be!*
> *When we all see Jesus,*
> *We'll sing and shout the victory!*

One thing, in fact, does last forever. It is your eternal soul, the part of you at the core of your innermost being. The question is, *where* will your soul last forever? If you arrive at the end of this life, whenever that may be, without Jesus, nothing else will matter. Nothing. It is the most important decision of your life, of your very eternal existence. As our Lord Jesus encourages us,

"But seek first the kingdom of God and His righteousness, and all these things shall be added to you" (Matthew 6:33).

God was guiding us to set our sights farther into the countryside, to another place to call home. I was getting less and less attached to what we had built on the hill. Some things were beginning to need maintenance, which I knew was an ongoing thing for every homeowner. But it added fuel to the fire that was kindled inside me to get us moving to the next place God had in mind for us to live, wherever that would be.

12

Pursuing Homelessness

The rich rules over the poor,
And the borrower is servant to the lender.
Proverbs 22:7

Selling our home was going to be hard, but we didn't know it at the time. We thought it would be a piece of cake. We had sold homes a couple of times before without a realtor, and had always found success in a reasonable timeframe. Since I had developed some marketing skills at work, I figured I had it down at that point, and when the masses discovered the best house on the planet was available, there would be people lined up at the front door with buckets of cash. I was so proud of the description on my for-sale-by-owner flyer:

Boasting one of the largest wraparound porches in the area, sit and enjoy the breeze while you watch the wildlife play. Soothe yourself in the Jacuzzi tub by starlight with a picture-window view. Storage includes a walk-in attic the full length of the garage! Enjoy dining while you watch the panoramic view of the great outdoors year-round.

Who could resist, right? I built an amazing for-sale-by-owner sign that we put out front, complete with a box in which to place our flyers. I believe the neighbors and busybodies around the neighborhood must have thought highly of my flyers, because they went like hotcakes. But then nothing happened—silence. The phone didn't ring, except for realtors wanting to list the house.

When we realized our sell-it-yourself effort would not work, we hired our first realtor. We thought if we could just hire one of the best realtors in the area, she would bring buyers in droves. She came, took tons of professional pictures, and put our house on the front page of the real estate section of the paper. But the droves never came. The contract expired, along with our hope for greener pastures.

Our house on the hill we had built was unique, so it would require a very special buyer. The average family of four, those who were ready for an upgrade to a bigger house, didn't appear to be interested in our six bedrooms, four bathrooms, and three levels. Sure, we had several offers along the way, but most of those were broker dealers who wanted to buy our place for an insultingly low price.

When God told us to sell our place, we thought it meant we were being some sort of super-obedient children of His. We surely had notions that because we had heard from God, He would send someone waltzing up the driveway carrying a sack of money to make us a full-price offer that couldn't be refused. It never happened. If the money-bag holder came to see us one day, we were either out back playing in the woods or off looking at a piece of property we couldn't afford. Speaking of which, during our lengthy sales process, which took years, we would occasionally look at some property here or there for our future place. But it was nothing serious. House and land hunting became a leisurely pursuit in our spare time, sort of like our hobby.

By 2016, we had become known to all our friends and family as the people with the house for sale. It had been on the market for not just months, but around three years. It always came up in conversations, with everyone asking if we had sold the house yet.

That year, 2016, brought with it a sense of urgency and a renewed spirit: we were selling and moving on, no matter what! One important note: we were like most people pursuing the American Dream. After being in that house for over ten years we had accumulated *stuff*, and lots of it. We had a shed full of stuff, oversized closets in every bedroom full of stuff, and a walk-in storage room over the full length of our garage full of stuff. We were one big happy family, and all eleven of us had created quite a collection of things.

It became clear that it wasn't just the house that God wanted us to let go of: it was our stuff, too. We soon became aware that if God wanted us to move somewhere smaller, we could not take all those things with us. After our own poor attempts to sell the house, we set out to hire an auctioneer to see if we could not only sell the house but also liquidate a whole host of things we determined needed to go. Auction fever took us over, and I had the worst case of it. The kids and Katrina became fearful of things they held near and dear to their heart being carried to the auction pile in the garage. There was weeping and gnashing of teeth for certain!

The auctioneer was determined to sell our house and many of the things we'd accumulated. The house had to reach a minimum reserve price to sell, but it was "anything goes" for most of our dearly held possessions. We were told it would be best for us to leave the property while the auction took place, so one fine spring day, we went up to our favorite park on the hill and let the kids play while all our stuff was rummaged through and sold.

Our most important reason for the urgency of this auction was to move forward in obedience to God. But unfortunately, the house didn't sell, not even close to the reserve price we had set. While most of the personal property sold and was hauled away when we returned, it was heart-wrenching to know we had essentially given most of that stuff away after we paid the auctioneer. In fact, we took a financial loss when it was all said and done. We were crushed in defeat. Had we heard the Lord wrong on this? We walked away from that experience bewildered and defeated.

In looking back on the auction, although it was a financial loss, I believe the two things that occurred were beneficial for us moving forward. One, it really made us take a hard look at our personal possessions and determine that we could, in fact, live without many of those things. Two, a significant portion of our stuff was now gone. While we could have spent several weeks or months having yard sales and selling online, it brought us to a place where we could let go of that stuff and move on, to set our sights on our next steps.

After the auction, we wasted no time signing a contract with a dear friend and successful real-estate broker. We had come to know Clint and his family through several activities and events with our church, as well as our homeschool community. In fact, while we'd been working through the auction process, he had helped us begin the property search anew. We really felt like it was not only time to move, but to move across the river, to another county that was closer to some strong, God-centered families whom we had come to love and appreciate. We became laser-focused on heading north, feeling like that was our new promised land. We had property hunting fever like nobody's business!

Frequent trips, especially on the weekends, brought us to random houses or properties that could possibly be candidates for our future home. In addition to Clint keeping us informed of any properties that came on the market, we became quite acquainted with all the real-estate search engines. I had it down to an art. Anything that had ten acres or more (within reason) was what we longed for. We weren't sure what we would do with it all, but we would figure that out once we arrived there. We even considered crossing the state line into Oklahoma if the right place came along.

We looked at newer houses, run-down houses, abandoned houses, and various other pieces of land that were undesirable for one reason or another. We drove out into the middle of nowhere and turned down what looked to be dead-end, one-lane dirt trails, only to find pitiful properties at the far end. Sometimes, we arrived at our destination and met hostile landowners who were angry because we'd wandered onto their private property. Usually, if a piece of property was ideal, either the price was too high or it was no longer available by the time we happened upon it. Years back, we had determined our wants and desires for the piece of paradise we were longing for, so it usually didn't take long to determine we were in the wrong place. We had a good idea of what we were looking for, and it needed to either have a creek running through it, a nice pond, or both.

We also learned that thorns can be good or bad. On one particular property we looked at, we discovered it was prime season for blackberries, one of our favorites. While out scouting the property, the kids sampled some of the beautiful berries, as they were in abundance. While discussing the property with the owner, we asked him about the berries and if he minded us having some. He didn't mind in the least, so we picked to our hearts' content. That was about the only good thing that came of that piece of property: a nice load of berries for a cobbler. Those were the good thorns.

On another property across the state line, we arrived at what appeared to be End-of-the-World, Oklahoma. Having only seen abandoned structures and no sign of life, we took the map I'd printed and set out to explore. Not long into our adventure in that godforsaken place, we discovered a veritable thicket of thorn trees. We should have taken the hint from the thorns, but the weather was good and we had time to roam, so we pressed on, doing our best to navigate them. Having found the pond in the center of the land of a thousand cuts, we gave up and turned back. Happy to finally escape without too much bloodletting, we were getting close to leaving when our curiosity bested us: we just had to peek into the abandoned homestead the previous tenant had pieced together from scrap lumber. After going inside, we determined that some crimes may have been committed there, given the fact that all the remaining personal possessions were strewn about as if the FBI had performed a raid looking for evidence. We may have lingered there a bit too long as a sense of darkness fell upon us, which hastened us to make our escape. We crossed that one off the list as we drove away.

Having put our sights back onto Crawford County, Arkansas, we finally found it. It was nestled in the country, just a short drive from interstate access and down a well-maintained gravel road. At first glance, I was turned off. As the chief skeptic of our clan, it was my job to pass judgment once all the details were in. After arriving at the corner entrance of those forty acres, we could barely park our van between the road and the cattle gate. There it was, grown up in all its glory—an abandoned house, the original homestead where someone had staked their claim in the early part of the last century.

The original tenants—who had apparently built that humble shelter with their bare hands—were the inventive type, to say the least. Although the house was littered with all manner of remaining personal possessions here and there, the owners had been quite clever in all of the ways in which they'd included small, built-in shelves and a variety of nooks and crannies to store things. Nobody had lived there for years, other than varmints. I was looking for the exit before whatever evil had befallen that old place crushed me and everything in it into a heap of rubble. Quite frankly, it gave me the creeps, but my sweet helper from God, always the optimist, said, "We could make this work.

This could be our place to live while we build our new house in another spot."

As we hung on to the hope of our house selling, we had the idea that if we found the right place, we could buy a camper and live in it while we built our next dream home. It seemed to be a growing trend. We had good friends who had done that very thing and they had several more children than we did. If they could do it, we could, right?

Then we began to wander across those forty acres. Stepping away from that old relic of a house was the best thing we had done since our arrival. We set out to find a potential building site in that wild place. Katrina, the kids, and I were always up for an adventure in the woods, and that adventure was no disappointment. After that first visit, we determined to not cross that one off the list just yet.

After looking into the property further, we learned that the county road made a diagonal trek right through the forty acres. On the east side of the road was a hill and bluff line on roughly fifteen acres. It could be doable for a house on the hill, but we had already had our fill of living on a hill at that point, so we determined that portion of the property could be a candidate for dividing and selling. The prime location was the other twenty-five acres in the valley below, the place we fell in love with.

On another trip to the property, after we'd taken the time to understand the boundaries a bit more, we set out to explore further, to find the hidden treasures that awaited us. It was then we discovered that not only did the property have one creek flowing past the original homestead, but it fed into another larger creek on the southern end, deeper into the woods. Our discovery of two creeks made this place quite desirable, not to mention the abundance of trees in every direction.

Although that amazing property was flowing like a fountain with creek water, it had one problem—there was no municipal water available to the property. The old house had been connected to a well, but other than that, we had no clue what we would do for water. To make that work would rely on resurrecting the existing well or drilling a new one, neither of which would be an easy or cheap task. Could it be done? Yes, but it was not our preference. After digging into the water issue a bit further, we opted to accept the risk and make a low offer on the property.

Shortly after our most recent trip to our newly found promised land, we made an offer, which was accepted by the seller. Unfortunately, we learned in the process that the actual seller had recently passed away, and the person we were now negotiating with was a relative who lived clear across the country in Connecticut. Additionally, Clint informed us that the property had to go through probate before anything could settle, which would take a minimum of ninety days. That sounded okay with us since we hadn't sold our house yet and still had to come up with a plan to pay for the land. The offer stood and we waited—waited for our house to sell and for news on the property to settle.

Waiting was hard, but it gave us a breather. Surely, that was the land we'd been hoping for, the place we'd dreamed of. We made many more trips to the land, just to wander the place and enjoy some family getaways. We had in our mind that we were likely moving there, so we settled into the idea that it would be ours soon. Many discussions were had as to where a new house could be built, whether we should build a low-water bridge across the creek, or whether we could even buy that camper and move there immediately. We were on our way, except for one huge problem: our huge house still hadn't sold.

The heat of summer set in and we were in a holding pattern—no progress on the land, no progress on the house. Then in late summer, we began to get a few nibbles on the house that renewed our hopes. Another big issue with selling the house was always being on call for a house showing. Every time Clint wanted to make an appointment, we were supposed to be thrilled to upend our life and abandon the house for a while. Oh, and it always had to be immaculate, which was nearly impossible with all of us trying to get on with life. Who keeps their house looking like a museum all the time, anyway? Katrina and the kids took the brunt of that drudgery since I was off at work when the happy calls would come saying, "Someone wants to look at the house today." There were many times Katrina and the kids either went for a walk while the visitors came or climbed in the van and pulled into the cul-de-sac down the hill and sat in the air-conditioning while they waited to return home. Not an easy process, to say the least.

September of 2016 finally brought a ray of hope. That month, we began to have some repeat house lookers, people who had a keen interest in our place. We had a couple of families on the hook, neither of which was willing to pay top dollar, which was a downer for us. Still, through that entire process, we did not lose sight of the objective: to sell our house, downsize, move to the country, and obey God's leading. Nothing in that regard changed for us, no matter how long and painful the process. While I had named our ideal selling price years earlier to put us in a good financial position, we were nowhere close. But would we make a profit on the house? Indeed. As disappointing as it was to settle for less money, we finally accepted a *real* offer and proceeded with a contract on the house. Praise the Lord!

Our goal from the beginning was to sell the house to be free from the mortgage before moving on to our next place or a building project. In our two past experiences, moving and *then* selling our house had put us in quite a bind, requiring us to pay two mortgages for a time until the house sold. We would have to find a short-term rental. Neither of us had rented a place to live since before we'd married, so we had to reintroduce ourselves to the rental process. A house that could hold all our remaining possessions, our family of seven (our four oldest were out on their own at that point), a small dog, an outside cat, and a pen full of chickens and guinea fowl would have to be quite a find. We were starting to put the forty-acre property out of our mind: it seemed to be indefinitely delayed. We were still pondering what to do with that if something changed, but in the meantime, we needed a rental.

We were spoiled in our private location. Although we had neighbors, they were very good neighbors and far enough away that we seemed to live in our own private haven. Finding a place we deemed safe for our family was also a huge obstacle, not to mention our growing animal collection we had in tow. Days passed, and we were growing desperate to find a place with a looming closing date on the house. We had also been working nonstop packing, packing, packing, getting ready to move to who-knows-where.

Searching multiple online rental listings was tiring and options were limited. We had to keep in the back of our minds that some or all the animals might have to go elsewhere if we had to move without them. Then on a Friday afternoon, after being sick of looking at house rental listings, I just happened to catch a property out in the country that had only been listed online for about thirty minutes. I called immediately and the owner gave me a time the next day to look at the property. Things were looking up.

Somehow, we managed to be getting on with life amid all these struggles and trials. Before we knew we were moving we had scheduled a vacation, right in middle of when we'd likely have to be out of the house. Oh, and for the first time ever, I had been training to run a 10k race. I suppose some of those things could have been cancelled, but we were determined to push through it all and get to the finish line with the house, the vacation, and the 10k!

The next day, when we looked at the rental property, the owner was very nice and seemed happy to have us looking at the house. While the house wasn't the best and needed a few things done, it was in the perfect location. The house had a giant cow pasture behind it as far as the eye could see and another field across the road that was unused. We wanted to make a quick decision, but we had a few details to work out with the potential landlord. First, we wanted to know if we could build a chicken pen in the backyard to move the chickens into. Also, he insisted the house have no inside pets except for our fish aquariums. When we asked to bring our small dog along if we made sure to keep him outside, he agreed. We planned for him to come back by our house we were selling for us to sign a lease contract and give him our deposit and first month's rent payment.

Later that afternoon, when the landlord arrived at our house, we invited him in and he came and sat down at our dining room table. Right after we began discussing the details of the paperwork, our little Yorkie-Poo, Sammy, came in the room where we were. Normally, Sammy would have been yapping his head off at any stranger, but for some reason, he just came in the room and hopped up in the lap of the landlord.

"Is this the dog you were worried about having to build a pen for?" asked the landlord. "He seems like no problem at all. Y'all can just let him be in the house; he doesn't look like much trouble." Praise the Lord! God had used our little dog to soften the heart of this guy whom we had only met the day before. It was a huge relief knowing we didn't have to build another pen for Sammy. Problem solved!

The first of October rolled around, and we had a place to move and a short time to get there. We only had about three weeks ahead of us to run a marathon, and I'm not talking about my 10k. A chicken pen needed to be built, and everything we owned needed to be relocated to our newly found rental house. And in the middle of all that, we somehow needed to sandwich the vacation we had scheduled with Katrina's family. We determined to make the first two weeks of October our non-stop weeks, pouring everything we could muster into them so we could go on vacation, relax, then return for a final push of last-minute moving.

A dear friend and church member offered us his truck and trailer for as long as we needed it, an amazing blessing that we gladly accepted and took full advantage of. For the next week or so, Katrina and the kids would pack all day while I was at work. Then I'd come home and we'd load the trailer as full as we could get it, take the load to the new house, unpack, put things where we could, come home, go to bed, and repeat daily for two weeks until we were worn smooth out. Then we *absolutely* needed a vacation! Although we hated to step out of the middle of one of the most important events that had come our way in quite a long time, we embraced the chance to get away and take a break. It gave us some time to pause, swim, and recharge for the final sprint.

Everything seemed to be going as planned. After returning from our vacation, we built a large chicken pen at the rental house, I ran my 10k, and we moved the remainder of our things. We had a few delays with the buyer of our house near the end, but that gave us a little extra time for last minute things. We were moved into our new temporary dwelling at the rental with days to spare. God had given us a mind to work, a lot of help along the way, and a strength that allowed us to move what seemed like a mountain.

We had done it. We were free. For the first time in our marriage, we finally got a taste of what it meant to be truly debt free. No credit cards, car payments, medical bills—and now no mortgage. We now had some house money in the bank that would assist us with our future, although we didn't clearly know what that looked like yet. With God's amazing guidance every step along the way, we had moved off the hill God told us to move to in the first place, Stonebridge Hill.

A season of our life had closed, a chapter in our life completed. That day was exhilarating, walking away from the title office having just handed over the keys of our family home to someone else. For the most part, our five youngest children had never really known anywhere else. That house had been their life-long home, the place they had made most of their childhood memories to that point.

Yes, that was signing day, the day we walked through a door God had opened wide and invited us to step through. We were now turning the page in the book of our lives to a blank page, one that would require the boldness to put the pen to paper and follow the nudging and direction of our ready writer, God our Father. Wherever He led, we were ready to follow.

On to the next adventure.

13

In Search of Elsewhere

Looking back can be quite troublesome. Ask Lot's wife. She's a rather salty gal.

I have a small New Testament I used to keep on my desk at work, a gift someone had given me in years past. Many times, it just sat there as a reminder to always be in the Word, but at times, when I didn't have my full-size Bible with me, I would pick up that little New Testament and read a passage here and there, or something would come to mind and I would need to open it up to confirm a Scripture reference. I suppose I have been using it for the better part of twenty-five years.

Around the time we were going through all our land searching and moving away from Stonebridge Hill, I opened the Scriptures, not looking for anything in particular, and stumbled onto a short little verse in Luke 17. While Christ was teaching about His second coming, He emphasized the idea that when He returns, we must not look back to get some things in the house or to finish plowing the field. Then Jesus said, "Remember Lot's wife" (Luke 17:32).

For some odd reason, when I opened that little Bible to that page, the type made those three words stand out to me like nothing else was on the page. God was making it clear to me that when we look back to take hold of this world, it can be detrimental. In the Old Testament story, when God was rescuing Lot and his family from the destruction of Sodom and Gomorrah, the angel warned Lot and his family not to look back while escaping the region. Lot's wife, for whatever reason, looked back and became forever petrified—literally, as she was turned into a pillar of salt. That really brought relevance to the journey God had been taking us through. Don't look back. Let go. Press on.

The land across the river, the forty acres we had been pursuing while we had sold the house, fell through. To this day, we have not been back to the place to see what has come of it. What we do know is that we believe God saved us from a world of unseen grief and financial loss, things that may have been disastrous for us had we continued down that path. He made a way out and we knew it was time to put it out of our minds, which we did. We never looked back.

As we settled into our little rental house, a reasonably sized four-bedroom place in the country, it seemed to be exactly what we needed to put our life on pause, get ourselves together, and seek the next steps.

We had enjoyed wonderful privacy and good neighbors in our house on the hill, so we were very anxious about who we would be moving next to. When I say, "moving next to," I mean we were now in a house that was sandwiched between a house on either side, which was quite an adjustment for us. Little did we know that God had moved us into a short row of five or six houses in the country that were almost all owned by the same family. God had moved us next door to the Jones family, in both directions.

On one side was Mr. Jones, his wife, and his daughter. Mr. Jones was a Baptist preacher who was essentially the watchdog and overseer of our row of houses. On the other side of Mr. Jones was his brother-in-law. On the other side of us was Mr. Jones' grown daughter and her family. Oh, and by the way, Mr. Jones had built the house we were renting, one of the original houses in the row, so he knew all about the place, having sold it to our landlord in years past. There we were, right in the middle of one big happy family. Mr. Jones let us know we were safe and that he would keep an eye on our place while we were away. What a blessing!

Not long after getting settled into our little country rental home, we resumed our search for our next destination. When I say "settled," I mean we had everything under roof. One spare bedroom, as well as the entire garage, was stacked with boxes of our stuff from floor to ceiling, wall to wall. We settled into the remaining three bedrooms: one for Katrina and me, one for the boys, and one for the girls. All our bedrooms were stacked with boxes in every space we could find along the walls. While it was not ideal, keeping everything crammed in the house kept us from having to rent a storage facility until we moved and gave us instant access to our stuff whenever we needed to find something. It was messy, but we made it work.

As our full-time hobby of conducting property searches resumed, we began to open our minds a bit but still stayed focused on the main things we had listed for our dream property: a nice place in the country, acreage, a pond, a creek, and the promise of minimal to no debt. I kept in close contact with our realtor and between the two of us finding properties, it seemed we were running to look at places every spare moment we had. It wore us out again!

We had been in the rental for almost two months. Thanksgiving came and went; December was almost upon us. We had much to be thankful for and were continually seeking the Lord in prayer to give us clear direction. Our church family and other close friends, as well as family, were constantly lifting this burden of our next move up to the Lord. We had been on this journey of wandering through the wilderness for years, and although we had experienced the huge blessing of selling, we were getting impatient about getting to the promised land.

About a week after Thanksgiving, I stumbled upon a new property. Although I had never been to the place, I knew the couple who had built the house and knew it to be quite a nice home. While it had a few quirky things that were not exactly what we wanted, it was very well made and came with some land and room to expand, along with privacy in the country. Oh, and one more thing: an out-of-budget price. We were getting tired of waiting. As we sought the Lord, we asked Him to guide us to the right place and protect us from our own selfish desires, impatience, and excessive debt.

The next day, after we had determined in our hearts to go and look at the newer house that didn't fall within our debt reduction goals, we were close to calling Clint and having him set up an appointment. As with most anything, once a person gets their sights set on something wonderful, be it a house, car, or any other purchase, it's hard to settle for something less. Once your expectations get adjusted to that higher level, it blocks out logic and drives your emotions to make poor decisions. I was concerned that once we saw that place we would fall in love and then call the bank to climb back into the debt hole we had just climbed out of. Then God intervened.

That night, when we were about to set up an appointment to look at the house, my friend Kevin gave me a call. Kevin and his family have been instrumental in helping us along the way, and that day was no different.

"Hey," Kevin said, "I have a lady I work with who was telling me about a house down in Hartford, one that might be perfect for you."

I knew the place he was talking about. I had looked at it online every time I did a property search for the past several months. It had been out of our search range because it was in a part of the county we had deemed unacceptable for various reasons, one of which was our concern about personal safety. But the short conversation with Kevin that night led us to put things on hold and think things through.

The next day I called Clint to set up an appointment to look at a house, but it wasn't the new, expensive house. We decided to follow up on Kevin's suggestion and see the clunky-looking house that looked like it had been abandoned out in the farthest and worst part of the county. It was surely a bad sign when Clint called me back and said the listing agent didn't have time to show it to us and that she just gave him the lockbox code, which he passed on to us. Because Clint lived about an hour away from the house anyway, he encouraged us to check it out and let him know if we needed further assistance. I gave the code to Katrina, and she and the kids went to look at the house that afternoon while I was at work.

It was early December, which meant it would be dark by the time I left work. Nevertheless, Katrina called me to say I should meet them at the house so I could look. She said I was going to love it. I had heard the words, "You're going to love it!" many times by then, so that put up roadblocks in my mind immediately. Still, I agreed to meet them at the house.

I left work and drove, and drove, and drove, nearly to the end of the earth. Along the way, I passed properties and side roads that we had already determined were so far out of our driving range, we would never consider looking there. Not a good sign to me, especially in the dark, but I finally arrived at the potential dwelling place.

Katrina and the kids happily met me at the front door and welcomed me into the darkness, and with a small flashlight and our cellphone lights, we examined the place. Oh my! It was overwhelming, to say the least, as signs of abandonment and abuse dripped from every crevice. The place was a wreck. I walked around with my tour guide Katrina, letting her point out all the wonderful things about the place. She needed to do that for me, the skeptic, because I couldn't find any.

There were too many windows to count that were broken or damaged, the clawfoot tub in the master bathroom had fallen over, and dirt was mounded up where the tub drain was supposed to be connected, likely caused by some unknown varmint. The master bathroom seemed like a giant locker room for a ball team, the carpeting was atrocious, the kitchen bar and cabinets were a mess, and the tile throughout most of the place would have to be replaced. And that was just the first visual inspection in the dark. You can be sure that when I went back later in the daylight, the list grew much longer. The place looked like a dream house—for someone who wanted to spend the remainder of their days repairing it.

I took note of a few things that week, though, things that moved us in a new direction. Katrina was beginning to cross things off her "want" list. No garage? No problem. Ugly paint? She would paint it. Dilapidated deck? We'd replace it. Virtually everything we came up with as an excuse to not get the place Katrina just ignored. Perhaps our property searches over the past couple of years had numbed us to the potential in a place, but from building our dream home to walking away from it, God had moved in our hearts, especially Katrina's, to really accept things and improve them if possible. Although the place had a nice pond and ample acreage, there was no creek for her and the kids to play in. That was a bummer. We later learned that one of the most substantial creeks in the county, one that feeds the county water supply, ran through the neighbor's property just across the field.

After further digging, Clint learned that the place had been vacant for over three years, meaning it had gone back to the bank, a repo. Fortunately, we had hired the right agent, because Clint had a great deal of experience buying repossessed properties and restoring them, which really assisted us in the process. God could have given us any agent, but He put just the right one in our path whom we had come to know quite well, someone who would had our best interests in mind. After pondering the place for several days, it was time to assemble our multitude of counselors, friends, family, and church family who had walked alongside us on this journey.

Our parents came and gave the place a good look, pointing out many of the good and bad things and offering their advice. Our church family, who meets in each other's homes, were meeting in our rental house on an ideal Sunday in early December. After church, we all loaded up and travelled to the potential property together, about ten minutes away, for them to give us their advice about the place. While they shared our own reservations, they still overwhelmingly approved. As we walked through the grassy field on that cool, sunny December afternoon on our way back from the pond, I'll never forget the look on our friend Tony's face. As we walked along, he turned, looked me in the eye, and with confidence said, "This is awesome! This is the place we have all been praying about for years."

With a confident thumbs-up from our friends and family, and especially from our God, we proceeded to the next steps of working out the details of making an offer. After thoroughly looking over the place and hiring a house inspector, we determined where to begin the negotiation process with the seller, which was a bank holding company in New York. This meant we were dealing with someone from a distance who likely did not care about our timetable or desires.

During the week of Christmas, we made an offer on the house, and thus began the waiting and bargaining process. The holidays certainly put some delays in the mix, but over the next couple of weeks, having worked out some counteroffers and other details, we settled on a price that would put us on the fast track to getting out of debt. In less than a month, we had gone from almost falling headlong into much more debt on a newer house to securing a reasonable home that would take us in a good direction financially.

In the last week of January 2017, we signed the papers on a house that we could not even move into yet, given the number of improvements required to make it livable. We didn't care. We were elated. We left the title company that day in celebration, knowing we had waited, applied God's sound money principles, and consulted people of God who loved Him and us to bring us to a good place. We could have paid cash for the property with some inventive money juggling, but we had a real peace about getting a small, reasonable loan that would allow us to make much-needed improvements prior to moving in.

Thus began the remodel of our "new" farmhouse. We were almost home.

14

Almost Home

I t was the end of January 2017. Still living in our rental
house under the watchful eye of the Joneses, we had taken
the next step toward owning a place of our own. Yet taking
ownership of a piece of property can be intimidating, especially
given the seriousness of the signing event and the enormous stack
of papers that say, "Sign here." It's hard not to feel skeptical and
reluctant, wondering if you are inadvertently signing your life
away. Still, we left the title company that day with a pile of papers
in hand, a commitment to a relatively small mortgage to pay off
as quickly as possible, and the hopes of remodeling a farmhouse
that we could call home. It felt good. It felt right.

Something was different, though. This place didn't have
that new house feel (or smell) like when we had built our dream
house from the ground up. The house was essentially uninhabitable unless all we were looking for was a roof over our heads.
It had issues and we knew it, but that was what we had signed

up for. It wasn't just the newness, though: something else felt different this time. Nonetheless, a nice cup of coffee to celebrate was in order, so after the signing event, I made a pit stop on my way back to work, stopping at a local coffee shop to obtain some soothing, dark-roast black java.

Coffee in the cupholder, I made the short trek across town back to work to finish out my day. As I drove, my mind was racing with the details of the past several weeks as well as the years leading up to the defining moment we were living through. We were stepping out into a new direction, heading out into the country to develop a new life. I'm not going to lie. Our "new" house was a mess, and I knew I would be the lead contractor for all the repairs. Yet my thoughts were not on the details of what to renovate first. The Lord was sharing some new information with me, taking me in a new direction.

Let me pause at this moment to interject another part of the journey. One thing we had been praying for, in addition to starting a farm and developing the country life, was the chance to detach from my corporate job of twenty-four years, which was getting more stressful as each year passed, sucking the life out of the family and me. In the first part of January, the company offered senior employees a buyout to leave the company forever. That sounded like a dream! We were so close to being debt-free we could taste it. Although signing onto a small, short-term mortgage was a necessity at the time, the debt was certainly weighing heavy on us during all our emotional wranglings. I was literally offered the opportunity to leave the company and get paid my full salary for a whole year. However, the stipulation was that I could never return to work there.

Oh my, was that job buyout ever a huge temptation, one that I perceived as a once-in-a-lifetime opportunity to walk out, start a new life, and move in a new direction, away from the corporate environment. So many decisions to make in such a short time— we needed a serious word from the Lord to ensure leaving the company, in addition to taking on that new house project, was what we needed for our family. After much prayer and consideration with our always-present godly friends and family, we all came to the consensus that none of us had any peace about me leaving my work at that time.

I wrote some notes about the process in my journal:

Mid-January, 2017

After praying and talking with a few folks this past week, unless we hear a direct word from God to leave my work, I think we should stay. As much as Katrina wanted me home and I wanted to be home, we felt the same: no peace.

God can certainly move us in a direction away from my current work any time He wants. He can and will provide all our needs beyond anything we can imagine. We will wait for Him.

Waiting is such a pain, isn't it? Who really likes to wait? Nobody in our culture, that's for sure, including me! We are all so used to driving up, ordering a cheeseburger, pulling up to the window, and driving away with something to eat—which hardly counts as food. But we all know waiting can pay off: going to a good restaurant with a nice atmosphere and lingering over a long dinner means a much better meal. Waiting for the right thing is always worth it.

In the book of Isaiah, the prophet emphasizes how the Lord comforts His people, caring for them in their difficulty. The oft quoted crowning verse concludes the chapter well:

But those who wait on the Lord shall renew their strength;
They shall mount up with wings like eagles,
They shall run and not be weary,
They shall walk and not faint.
Isaiah 40:31

As for me, I have always thought of this verse as the one people put next to a picture of an eagle soaring high above the mountains. It seems like that has caused me to glaze over it and not really capture the extent of the entire verse and chapter. Those of us who have been in the church for any length of time tend to get numb to many of the commonly quoted verses of our faith.

This verse is not just about soaring like the eagles. It is about waiting. When we wait, we will be refreshed not only in spirit, but literally, in the physical sense. If we clamor through life expecting everything to show up in front of us instantly, the growth that comes from waiting is missed. The appreciation for the Provider is forgotten.

Have you ever been to a child's birthday party where the star of the show isn't much of a star? They sit in the middle of the excitement, presents all around, with the hopeful glee of a pig in the trough. One gift after another is gobbled up, wrapping paper strewn about, and as the onlookers watch in amazement, nothing seems to be appreciated. Is it any wonder that when a child finally reaches the adult years, they have no use for a God who makes them wait for things? God is crazy about them, but because they expect every day to be like their last dozen or so birthdays, they just check out and chase after the world instead of following God.

Many of us are like that child. We want what we want, and we want it now. We throw our own little fits at times. No waiting for me, thank you very much!

God told us to *wait* on that work opportunity. Just like we had to wait for years to obtain the farm property, we were going to put our focus on the property first, among other things, then wait to see what the Lord would develop in my work. No early retirement for me. At least, not yet.

During the trip from the title office via the coffee shop, God began pouring ideas into my mind, things that were coming so fast I had a hard time taking them in.

The place we were at in life did not just happen overnight. Those events were a culmination of a lifetime of experiences, things the Lord had brought us through to teach us to trust Him, to wait on Him, and to shift the focus from ourselves to Him.

Through all our years of growing up in the church, we had heard all about Heaven: that we would be going there, that this life is temporary. Perhaps when you are a younger person, eternity doesn't seem relevant, like it is some faraway time that will only happen after you get old and pass from this life. I have to say, the older I get (and I am still quite young!), the more I long to escape this crazy life and enter the promised land.

Up until a few years prior, our lives had been consumed with building our castle, our heaven on earth, our American Dream. We could justify that our space was needed due to our large family, but in the past, families crowded into small spaces and made the best of things. That is how our parents and the generation before them grew up, squeezing in and making do with what they had.

As I was driving, the thought came to me that we should name our new place Almost Home Farm. This would indicate it was not going to be our dream home or our forever farm, that it would be just our temporary dwelling for now, our "almost" home. That seemed fine to me, especially since there were several things about the new farmhouse I loathed, given its state of disrepair at the time. Nevertheless, I drew a logo for our future farm, a large capital "A" connected at the bottom with a large capital "H." At the bottom right corner of the "AH," I drew a circle leaving the bottom of the "H," circling the top of the letters counterclockwise, turning back underneath the bottom, then forming an arrow pointing upward to the right of the "H," indicating that we should be thinking about things in an upward direction, our future home in Heaven:

I began writing down songs that spoke to me about this concept from several hymns and Christian music artists. God put the verses from Jesus in my mind about the many mansions He is building for us in Heaven:

> *Let not your heart be troubled; you believe in God, believe also in Me. In My Father's house are many mansions; if it were not so, I would have told you. I go to prepare a place for you. And if I go and prepare a place for you, I will come again and receive you to Myself; that where I am, there you may be also. And where I go you know, and the way you know.*
> John 14:1-4

The day after the house signing, I was torn between which house to call Almost Home since we lived in a rental that was undesirable and had just bought a farmhouse that was uninhabitable. That required us to set our sights on getting very, very busy. We wanted to be out of the rental house as soon as possible, not only because we were ready to be in our new home, but because we were tired of throwing away money on rent. Thus began another very busy season for us.

We were Almost Home.

15

Cultivating

To everything there is a season,
A time for every purpose under heaven.
Ecclesiastes 3:1

The book of Ecclesiastes, one of my favorite books of the Bible, is a wonderful collection of the musings of Solomon, the wisest man who ever lived. Solomon had obtained a most generous and wonderful gift from God, the gift of wisdom, and spent the remainder of his days using that gift to the amazement of people from nations near and far. The natural consequences of his fame brought him prosperity beyond measure, and at the end of all his days, in the book of Ecclesiastes, Solomon discusses the fact that we accumulate possessions our entire lives, enjoy the fruits of our labor, and then when we are no more, everything we have worked for becomes the property of another. The size and variation of our modern heaps of stuff may be different, but those things that remain here when we are dead and gone will no longer be of concern to us. Nobody escapes this inevitable conclusion.

In the dead of winter, at a place in the country on the edge of nowhere, was the dilapidated farmhouse of which we were now the proud owners. The list of needed improvements for the interior alone was long and broad; our priorities just had to be put in proper perspective to determine where to begin. Outside, the yard, bushes, trees, and shrubs needed serious attention to make the place look like a home again. Our first task was to make the place livable so we could move there as quickly as possible and get our new farm life moving along, while at the same time not rushing things too fast. We needed to pace ourselves.

Right after we closed on the property, Katrina and kids were excited to get out to the farm to begin cleaning things up and see what needed doing while I was at work. Since the house had been vacant for years, it seemed to have drawn the attention of folks in the vicinity, as people had apparently come to the house to hang out or just look around at times. Some had been there to steal and destroy, as all the electrical fixtures on the outside were completely gone. It left things looking pretty sketchy.

On the day Katrina and the kids arrived at the house to work for the first time, they were surprised to find an older man who had decided to come to the house to hang out that day. As they arrived, they discovered he had fallen and hit his head, which was bleeding, and that he was out of sorts. He claimed he was waiting for someone to arrive with the key and that Donald Trump had given him the house. Katrina told him it was our house, but that did no good since he wasn't in his right mind, so she and the kids left immediately. They drove to the closest neighbor, whom we had never met, and the neighbor called her son-in-law, who just happened to work for the local police department. Before long, the police, sheriff's deputies, and an ambulance had shown up to see what was going on.

Once the authorities arrived, Katrina and the kids went back to the house to see if they were getting things sorted out. The paramedics were treating the elderly gentleman, who was not himself. Apparently, he had become out of sorts from some of his medication and had driven from his home a few miles away to our place. While it seemed creepy to have a stranger camping out on our new front porch, he turned out to be harmless. The police and deputies hung out with the kids, letting them sit in their cars and play with the sirens and such—all was well.

That was the exciting welcome to our new country neighborhood. We asked ourselves, *Lord, why on earth have you brought us here?* We still ask that question at times, but not as much as we used to. Now that we have several years under our belt on the farm, we have seen God's providence work in so very many things. He is still moving, and it is always exciting.

One thing that God's hand was in was our remodeling adventure. We had built a house and many other things before, but those things take time, money, and expertise, and we wanted to make the best of all those things. It seemed like a scary proposition to just hire anyone to come to our house and be there with Katrina and the kids for days on end while they all worked on the place, especially after our scary beginning. Thankfully, we connected with a respected remodeling contractor named Bob, who was highly recommended by a friend.

Bob wasn't going to do everything, just some of the major things we couldn't tackle ourselves. We soon were moving along, and once Bob settled into the work at our place, he brought along another guy who worked with him. We were pleasantly surprised to learn that as they worked, Bob and the other guy talked about God off and on all day. We later learned they were both preachers on Sundays and did remodeling during the week. We were pleased God had provided a couple of first-class, upstanding gentlemen to do wonderful work on our home.

Between the remodelers and us, we began working ourselves to death. We were out at the house every day and night doing something to improve our new place. Our existence was consumed with getting up, going to work, working on the house all evening and weekends, going to bed, and repeating. The process reminded me of Solomon's words in Ecclesiastes 3, except with a bit of a twist:

It was a time to tear down walls
And a time to build new ones.
It was a time to chip up tiles
And a time to lay new ones.
It was a time to clean off walls
And a time to repaint.
It was a time to pluck up
And a time to plant.
It was a time to pull down
And a time to build fences.

It was a time to remove windows
And a time to install new ones.
It was a time to dig trenches
And a time to install water lines.
It was a time to pull out old wires
And a time to install new fixtures.
It was a time to remove cabinets
And a time to install new ones.
It was a time to rent
And a time to move in.

Three months flew by in a hurry, and we were dead tired. At that point we had been in our temporary house for almost six months, which was only ten minutes from the farm. Nonetheless, our heart was at the farm, and the six-month mark seemed like the opportune moment to get out from under the dreaded rent we hated paying each month. Although the work at the house was not complete, it was now livable, so we shifted gears into getting moved as quickly as possible.

At the end of April 2017, we bid farewell to the rental house and made our permanent residence at the farm, finished or not. We lacked a few appliances and some other things, but with two functional bathrooms (and one still being remodeled), we made the best of things with a microwave oven, electric skillet, and toaster until we had the oven, stove, and kitchen sink installed. We survived just fine with minimal cooking. Perfect or not, we were now residents of a farm.

The spring weather and growing stability on the farm let Katrina and I get back to walking again. We had been killing ourselves working on the house, which seemed like good exercise, but we wanted to get back to our routine of walking in the morning since it was not only good for our bodies, but for our relationship. We soon learned we could go a few different directions from our front door and down a country road or two, so that worked out well.

Getting out early in the mornings before I had to leave for work began giving us exposure to some of the neighbors and their routines as well. Nobody walked or exercised much on these country roads, but we soon became acquainted with our closest neighbors, the Ellisons. Doug Ellison and his family lived across the field to the west, and his elderly mother, Mrs. Ellison, lived across the highway to the south of us. During our morning walks, we realized Doug and his mom had a religious routine of getting out at the break of dawn every day and driving up and down the roads in his farm truck to check on their cows in various fields. They were very interesting to us, and I know we must have seemed quite curious to them as well.

On many of our walks, as Katrina and I discussed the challenges of the day, one thing Katrina kept musing over was the huge creek across the field from us, between our house and Doug's. One of the things we were disappointed about when we settled for this house was that we would have no creek on our property. It was a big letdown, but one we were willing to live with as God guided us. Katrina had been praying for the courage to ask the Ellisons if we could visit their creek, but somehow, it never seemed like the right time.

Many times, Doug and his mom would stop and chat a little when they passed us on our walks, Mrs. Ellison being the main conversationalist. As they warmed up to us, it became a little more commonplace for them to stop and talk. Katrina, continually looking for an opportunity to ask them about visiting the creek, just never could seem to find the right moment. One day, in early summer, we were out for our walk as usual and there came Doug and his mom. After a brief conversation with them, Mrs. Ellison leaned out the truck window and, with a joyful twinkle in her eyes, said, "Y'all ought to get those kids over to the creek. They would love getting in that cold water this summer. Y'all are welcome to it anytime you like."

We were speechless.

In all our time of looking and waiting for just the perfect property, the one with a beautiful creek running through it, we could never make it happen in our own strength. Then one day, God sent a friendly, sweet widow and her son, the woman who had settled this area decades earlier, whose family came with the clear intention of settling on a good water source. Within a moment, God had opened her heart and her mouth and blessed us with access to a creek that didn't belong to us in the least. We have enjoyed it immensely ever since, as well as our relationship with the Ellison family. Good neighbors are priceless! We are blessed with many.

Now that we were the proud owners of a farm, the urge was upon us to live like farmers. To live like farmers, we would need to do what a farmer does—drive a tractor. But we had a more immediate need for something that could cut our waist-deep yard, which had been out of control for years. Being a warm-blooded American male, one who had never owned (or needed) a riding lawn mower even as I neared the mid-century mark, I determined a zero-turn mower was to be our first major purchase. It was an amazing investment, but little did I know I would soon be robbed of all the time I could spend on that mower. Our three girls, excited as I was to have a mower, took over that task and have been doing it ever since, praise the Lord!

We managed to get the yard under control in our first year, but our fields were another story altogether, which brought us back to the subject of a tractor. Given that we had settled there to pursue a debt-free existence, it made no sense to go into debt to buy a tractor and brush hog. We would have to revisit that at a later date. Since we had developed a growing relationship with our neighbor, Doug, I determined to swallow my pride and ask if I could pay him to use his tractor and brush hog. It was late fall that first year and Doug had several tractors. He was more than happy to help us out, even driving the tractor right over. He climbed off, pointed out a couple of things about the tractor, and told me to just keep it for a while, that he wouldn't be needing it.

What a blessing from the Lord! Here we were, new to the area, and we were quickly learning about the generosity of our neighbors. Giving me some time to keep the tractor allowed me to take my time in getting our property cleaned up nicely. I was able to take some time off work over the course of a few weeks and spend some quality time out on that tractor, just me, God, the wide-open field, and the sky. It was exhilarating. The memories of my childhood days learning to drive tractors in the hay-field flooded through my head as I drove along without a care in the world. Ah, the life of a farmer!

Gardening on the farm was on a whole new level compared to the worthless patch of ground we attempted to develop on our old hill. We were now living on flat, fertile soil, fresh new ground that seemed to have never been worked, at least not recently. In addition to being good soil, there were hardly any rocks. Now, I've lived in Arkansas most of my life, having dug holes and various things, and I have experienced rocks almost everywhere I have been. But not here. It has been a real blessing to be able to put a shovel or posthole digger into the ground without the back-breaking labor of excavating rocks.

We started gardening from scratch, tilling the grass-covered ground and pulling out piles and piles of grass and weeds, and we have been gardening ever since. Most of the kids were excited about growing their own stuff, especially when they learned they could do the work, grow their crops, sell them, and keep the money. They have learned real lessons as they have become entrepreneurs, figuring out what works and what doesn't. They have also reaped the rewards of growing vegetables to share with our family, bringing their bounty into the kitchen for all to enjoy the fruits of their labor.

In our first year, we established a garden, put our house in pretty good order, and whipped our fields into the best shape they had been in years. That prepared us to move forward with some animal projects. To that point in our lives, we had just been piddling with animals, but now that we had been blessed with room to grow, it was time for everyone who had a desire to experiment and pursue their interests. When we moved onto the farm, we only had our little house dog, chickens, ducks, and guinea fowl. As time went on, the ranks grew to include rabbits, a huge flock of chickens, more guineas, Great Pyrenees herd dogs, barn cats, a bottle-fed calf named Cheeseburger, goats, and a growing herd of sheep. We even allowed our oldest son and daughter-in-law, who lived just fifteen minutes away, to move their two horses onto our fields when the grass was plentiful. We had animals galore!

So, what made all this work? Hard work and diligence. We instilled in the kids from day one that every animal that belonged to them was their responsibility. They were the ones who would care for the animals, feed and water the animals, and buy their feed. It has been a real blessing watching them all in action. It never seemed like a chore for them. They took ownership of everything they had to take care of and just did the work. Rain or shine, cold or hot, they have done it with no hesitation. These kids have really learned to work, which has been one of our greatest desires.

Living on a farm was, for the most part, all that was needed to teach the kids the concepts of procreation. They saw animals in action and learned how God created them, and we all witnessed and assisted in the birthing of puppies, kittens, piglets, chicks, goat kids, lambs, guinea keets, and baby bunnies. There were times when we were having multiple live births of different types of animals all in the same week, one right after another. It was an exciting journey, to say the least!

In addition to the excitement of new life on our thriving farm, we saw animals die. Many times, a birth or illness would take the life of an animal, and we would all hang our heads in defeat. But in that defeat, we would all (especially the kids) lift ourselves up and do what needed to be done to get on with things. They all experienced the joys of life and the defeat of death and illness. Those are invaluable things that cannot be taught from a textbook or a classroom. Real life is the best teacher. There is a time to be born and a time to die.

We finished our first few years on the farm very tired and very satisfied. Some things in our grand experiment failed, while others thrived. Some things we changed, and others we abandoned. We were living joyfully, rejoicing in our work and God's bountiful blessings, as King Solomon knew was best: "I know that nothing is better for them than to rejoice, and to do good in their lives, and also that every man should eat and drink and enjoy the good of all his labor—it is the gift of God" (Ecclesiastes 3:12-13).

Yet, in all our enjoyment of living on the farm and working in the soil, God was also doing a work in the soil of our hearts. Things had been changing for the better in our personal lives, but not in my work life. I was living with a continual unsettled feeling, as if I was sitting atop a fence with one foot on the farm and the other foot in the corporate world. While we had thought we could make it work that way, we knew we were in for a season of change. We knew it was coming; we just didn't exactly know when.

16

A Season of Discontent

Corporate culture has a way of becoming murky over time, especially as a company grows or becomes part of a merger with an even larger organization. Changes occur, including roles, responsibilities, and how things are done and managed. When I first entered the marketing world, I was responsible for managing the creation of literature, presentations, and customer-facing materials, areas in which I excelled. Over time, the role morphed into that of a business manager and less of a marketing expert. While it presented new challenges for my work, driving me to learn new things, it also began a phase of disconnection as I became less and less interested in the complex processes required to do my job every day.

Naturally, I was looking for ways to settle into what I thought could still be the long haul for us, to remain with this company until retirement. It was during that time of rapid change at work that we had been developing our small farm, which was located nearly twice as far from my work as before. My drive time changed from twenty minutes to thirty-five, though for a time I didn't mind it so much. The new route took me down a pleasant two-lane scenic byway which gave me some good thinking time. My previous route to work, although shorter, had become a bumper-to-bumper stress zone. Time was valuable to me, especially as we were getting our new home up and running, so I was looking for opportunities to improve how I approached things in my work life.

Toward the end of our second year on the farm, the human resources department at work began experimenting with new ways for people to work, which included an option for working from home part time. Because we had already been praying for a way for me to be home more and close to the family and our farm, I was one of the first to raise my hand for the new opportunity. Because I had already had the option to work from home as needs came up, it seemed like a no-brainer. Within weeks, I began working from home regularly for two days a week, which later became three after I proved my ability to seamlessly take care of demands remotely.

Moving out of the office gave us some newfound freedom at home and reduced commuting expenses and the wasted time of driving. Thus began a journey of figuring out when to work, how to work, and what a flexible schedule could look like. Because I have always been a stickler for schedules and start times, my self-imposed discipline had me logging in and out on time, as well as adhering to a strict eight-to-five schedule. But as time went on and we settled into a groove, I began adding flexibility to my day. When Katrina and I wanted to take a walk while the weather was good, we walked, and I just completed my work later. We created a new environment that seemed to soften my discontent with work, at least for a time.

There was one telling moment I took note of, though, in the fall of 2019. One of the new requirements for us business managers was to create a detailed presentation reviewing our previous year's results, as well as what we projected for the upcoming year. The presentations were to be given to an audience of our peers and the upper management of the company. I had been polishing my presentation skills for years at that point, and my style was to make a presentation meaningful by telling a story in the process. The premade templates and canned, repetitive slides that were provided for us to follow were meaningless to me. Because I'd been doing the job for years, I took the artistic license to present the material my own way, telling the story behind the portion of the business I was responsible for.

While my presentation skills, in-person and online, had been applauded for years by our sales colleagues and customers alike, the management was not impressed with what I put together this time. At the end of the presentation, my manager, who was the overseer of the annual event, gave me feedback that was unpleasant, yet enlightening. He said something like, "Well, there is no doubt you are the best storyteller in the room, but your presentation was lacking in some areas." While that was a very frustrating moment for me, I walked away from it taking note of his compliment. Although I hadn't met his expectations, the word "storyteller" rang in my ears.

The holidays came and went as usual, and we started anew with the year 2020. My dad and mom came for a visit in early

January, spending the night with us, which gave us some extra special time with them we hadn't had in a while. Through all my years and all my successes, my parents have always been by my side, rooting for me every step of the way. During their visit, God gave me a nudge to take Dad to my office and see my work. Even though I'd been working there for decades and they had seen the outside of our company, I thought it would be nice for Dad to see my office, the place I had spent so many years of my life, which he had heard so much about. Deep down, I was proud of my success and wanted him to see it for himself.

On a cool morning, the first Saturday in January, when the office was silent and dark, I brought Dad in and slowly gave him a tour of the office. Dad was slow and methodical, stopping at times to look at things or ask questions. When we arrived at my office, the place I was still spending two days of my workweek, I motioned Dad in and he sat down at my desk chair while I took the visitor chair.

Now, you must understand, my dad is quite hard of hearing. He has a difficult time carrying on a conversation with lots of people, especially when there is ambient noise. His hearing aids pick up the faintest of sounds, which distract him from being able to listen and converse well. But in my quiet office, with no one around, I had Dad's full attention.

We took some time to visit a while about my frustrations with work. I shared with him that my heart was not really in it and that we were looking for the next steps God had in store for us, whatever those looked like. He listened to me a lot and shared some stories from his own past that let me know he understood where I was coming from. I continued to share several things with him, and he confided in me some of his own concerns about his health.

After we finished talking and enjoying the moment there in my little office, we took each other by the hand, like a handshake, and held on firmly as we each prayed. Dad prayed for me and then I prayed for Dad, both of us lifting each other's concerns to the Lord. In all the years I had spent in that office pursuing success for my work, nothing compared to that moment there with God, Dad, and me. It was a monumental moment, priceless.

Not long after my dad and I prayed together in my office, things began to change at work. Katrina and I were beginning to see the writing on the wall. My time there would likely be coming to an end, not because I couldn't do the work, but because it would soon be time for me to move on, to pursue a calling in a new direction. That emboldened us to begin diligently praying that God would allow me to work from home full time. We didn't know what that looked like yet, but we prayed for it fervently. We had no idea how big the changes were that were coming, not only for us, but for the entire world.

For the most part, I had been working steadily at home three days per week and going to the office on Thursdays and Fridays. When special events or meetings came up at work, my work-from-home schedule took a backseat and I was required to be there in person, which was reasonable. Within weeks of our fervent praying, I was required to attend a series of special in-person work meetings related to our manufacturing facilities. There was an unsettled feeling during the time of those meetings, especially since the entire world seemed to be trying to figure out what was going on with a new virus called COVID-19. Before we knew it, the meetings were abruptly adjourned and our entire office was given orders to work from home until further notice. While I had no idea, nor did anyone else at the time, what this "virus" stuff was all about, the working from home part was music to our ears. God had come through for us, giving me a new way to work from home full time. God had answered our prayers!

Working from home became the new normal for me and everyone else at the office. What I had been doing part time for over a year had become everyone else's new full-time challenge. I was in heaven, though many of the others were not liking working from home one bit. While I had my lovely wife and five youngest kids to hang out with at home while I worked, many folks were alone. It began to shed some light on the fact that some people can thrive working from home, and others cannot. While I had acclimated to walking outside and checking on our goats or looking at the wide-open sky or mountains when I needed a break, I began to understand that some people long for that interaction at the coffee pot to make human contact. I was blessed with all the human interaction I needed, as well as the animals and the great outdoors.

The year 2020 rolled out with unprecedented changes and uncertainty, not only for our family and my work, but for the entire world. Our company stood tall, still meeting the expectations of our customers as most of the rest of the world was learning to do. But in the wake of everything that was going on, when all hell was breaking loose worldwide, Katrina and I, along with our church family, were still faithfully praying for positive change and direction for my work. We all knew (including a handful of my closest coworkers) that discontent had taken deep root in me, despite me getting to work from home one hundred percent of the time. While I was plugging away at work, day in and day out, Katrina, my ever-present counselor, knew I was not in a good place. Over the course of time, she had told me repeatedly I should just resign from my position at work and God would take care of us.

One highlight amid the chaos of 2020, when the world was falling apart, was paying off our mortgage in May of that year. There I was, working from home in a house that was paid for. We were totally debt free, having diligently applied God's financial principles for years, and the elimination of our mortgage took another level of pressure off. Still, despite Katrina's relentless support and faith in our God to provide for us, I did not have any peace about walking away from my work without a clear plan. I remained unsettled as we prayed through it, continuing to wait amid unprecedented uncertainty across the entire world. God had come through for us so many times before, and He would do it again in His good time.

17

Let the Rocks Cry Out

But He answered and said to them, "I tell you that if these should keep silent, the stones would immediately cry out."
Luke 19:40

During my time working from home, Katrina and I were especially good at taking our walks together. We weren't on a schedule, but when the time and weather were right, we headed down the road in one of a few directions from our doorstep. We loved being together in the great outdoors to walk, talk, and pray. One of our favorite destinations was James Fork Creek, which we also referred to as Shiloh Creek because we walked down a quiet country road, Shiloh Road, to get there. On Shiloh Road is the one-mile tree, a huge oak tree near the edge of the creek a mile from our house.

Over time, that place also came to be known as the Beaver Camp to us because the beavers were always busy in that area, chopping down shrubs and trees and dragging them to the water to build their structures. Although we spotted a beaver somewhere else along the creek one time, we never actually saw a beaver at the Beaver Camp. But oh, how they were busy, and they left their evidence all up and down the creek. One of my hobbies as we walked was to collect interesting-looking beaver sticks, sticks that had been hewn down and cleaned off nicely by the beavers. They made great walking sticks.

I also started looking for interesting rocks. The creek was full of thousands and thousands of rocks of various sizes and varieties that were washed, tumbled, and eroded over time as the seasons changed and the creek levels rose and fell. Looking for the ideal skipping rock was also a fun thing to do, and they were plentiful. On most of our walks, we wound up taking a load off, planting our backsides on a big rock or heap of rocks, and soaking in God's amazing beauty while we conversed. Sometimes, when I felt particularly lazy, I lay on my back and took in the blue sky and passing clouds through the massive trees above. I groped blindly through the scattered rocks in either direction, feeling for the ideal rock to send upward. When I found just the ideal projectile, I launched it almost straight up into the air, at hopefully just the right trajectory, and waited for the sweet *kerplunk* or *bloop* as it hit the pool in the creek just in front of us. It was important to be on high alert, mind you, because if my aim was poor, I sometimes put myself (or heaven forbid, Katrina!) in harm's way as the law of gravity kicked in and brought the rock back at my head. I was usually pretty good at it, but not always, which reminds me of something hilarious.

Remember the old black-and-white show *The Little Rascals* from the Great Depression era? We used to sit with our children and howl with laughter at some of those old Little Rascal episodes from yesteryear. Some of them are dumber than dirt, but you have to hand it to the creator who had such a vivid imagination: they were priceless. In one episode, one of the "rascals" is throwing rocks at a villain who has climbed up a telephone pole. After most of his rock tosses, the boy is unsuccessful and gets bonked on the head. Over and over, he throws the rocks, eventually hitting the bad guy. They don't make shows quite like that anymore!

Aside from throwing and skipping rocks, I also began looking for rocks that had a special meaning, an odd shape, or a message for me. I'm not sure why, but the pursuit became a game for us when we'd go on our adventures. We'd be going along and I'd spot a rock, pick it up, and ask Katrina, "What does this one look like?" She was less interested than me, but she was usually a good sport and would play along, saying what came to her mind.

One day in the spring of 2020, we were wandering across one of our usual rocky areas at the creek when I looked down, leaned over, and picked up an oddly shaped stone. The rock fit nicely in the palm of my hand: it was about three inches in length and a little over an inch wide. I suppose it was some sort of sandstone. On the top, it had two somewhat straight edges that formed a slight peak at the top. Its underside, opposite the two straight edges, formed a curve, like one of those old-world stone bridges going over a stream. As I continued to roll it around in my hand, it came to me—that rock looked like a tiny bridge. I took note of it, shoved it in my pocket, and went on to catch up to my lovely adventure queen, who was as usual wandering elsewhere down the creek.

Later that evening, as the family started gathering for dinner, I brought my prize rock out of my pocket, wondering what the kids would say it looked like. While we had one wiseacre at the table pipe up and say, "It looks like a rock," we labeled his vote as an outlier and told him, "No dinner for you!" But all the remaining clear thinkers at the table agreed, one by one, that it did indeed look like a bridge.

For years, Katrina and I have been interested in bridges. The sight of an old bridge off the beaten path has always generated excitement for us. On our honeymoon, there was an old bridge we stopped at to take some pictures of, which provided a beautiful backdrop to the spring waters rushing by underneath. While so many types of bridges exist and their architecture varies, there is one thing all bridges have in common—bridges connect things, making it much easier to travel to and fro, back and forth. They add value to our lives, not only in practicality, but in beauty as well.

I took note of the little bridge I was holding in my hand and placed it on the bookshelf, where it stood there as a reminder of our day at the creek. I later moved it to the tiny shelf by the chair in the sunroom where I started each day reading my Bible, thinking, and praying. I would pick up the little bridge occasionally, flip it around in my hands, and wonder, *Lord, what are you trying to tell me about with this bridge?*

One thing I was sure of: we had been praying, often and diligently. We were asking God to clearly reveal to us the direction we needed to go with my work, our farm, and our dream of a home business. Work had been continually wearing on me, but I hadn't seen a way out yet. I needed a crystal-clear exit strategy and a plan for where I would land afterward. But it wasn't coming to me. I was miserable in my job, but I continued to wait on the Lord.

June came, which in Arkansas brings increased heat and relentless humidity. Another thing June brought me was a dream. I would generally not consider myself to be a bedtime dreamer, and when I have them, they are usually a culmination of nonsense my brain has pieced together from recent experiences. The dream I had in mid-June was different. It was odd in some ways, but it was vivid and spoke to me with clarity. It caused one of those grab-the-journal-and-write-till-your-hand-falls-off moments:

June 17, 2020

I was riding along in a large bus, one of those buses used for touring around the country. The bus not only had normal seats, but it had tables and booths in it that you sit in, like a restaurant, or maybe something you see inside a camper trailer. I was sitting in the booth with several good friends from work, many of whom I recognized very well, whom I had worked with for many years. There were a lot of other people who filled up the rest of the bus. It appeared we were traveling, yet we were going nowhere in particular. As we sat in our booths, everyone was playing board games. We would ride the bus for a while and then occasionally stop at a large truck stop. Everyone would file off the bus and go inside, then stand in lines waiting to use the restrooms or whatever else we needed to do. Then we would assemble outside, load up on the bus, take our seats in our booths, and resume our journey to nowhere, playing our games as we traveled along.

What did the dream mean? From my perspective, I had been going to the same workplace every day for most of my adult life. I would get on the "bus" and spend all day with some wonderful people, and we would play games all day even though the games weren't that fun. The bus stopping for us to get off represented our commute home, our brief break from the bus. Then the next day, we would hop back on the bus and play games all day until the next stop. I was ready to get off that bus, to stop playing games, but I needed a clear plan on how to get there.

A week after my odd trip on the "dream bus," we went for another one of our journeys to the creek, just an ordinary morning walk to one of our favorite places, down to a river birch tree. We had become very acquainted with that familiar old tree. On one trip, I had carefully cut a large poison ivy vine off the trunk, partially rescuing the tree from the smothering vines that crept up to the highest heights of the gentle giant. At other times, we would sit on the huge roots that spread across the water's edge and formed a perfect bench.

That day was like so many others as Katrina and I sat down, enjoying the steady flow of the creek that made its way around a bend at the base of the tree. As we enjoyed the coolness of the morning, we prayed about some things together. After Katrina prayed, I turned my focus to the huge, clear water pool at arm's length, just in front of me, and prayed, "Lord, I pray that if I am to leave my job, would You please make it crystal clear to us? Make it as clear as this water in which I can see that brightly colored red and blue fish that seems to be looking up at me."

As we continued to pray, Katrina moved a little closer to have a look at the fish I was praying about. But my sights had moved from the fish to the trunk of the tree, where I could clearly see several stones deeply embedded in the wood. Over time, those stones had lodged there and the tree had engulfed them, making them permanent fixtures. In that very moment, God impressed upon me that I was like those stones embedded in the tree. The huge tree, which to me represented my employer, had essentially swallowed me up. My nearly thirty-year career there had become my prison, much like the embedded stones, and I was unable to escape.

I expect that most sane people, especially those who do not know the Lord, will put me in the category of "lunatic" at this point. Just wait—it gets better.

Picking Up Clues

In all my searching and seeking to find my contributions to this life, I have picked up on clues along the way and listened to others who have poured themselves into me. Listening to others is crucial to our walk in this life. God puts people in our lives to train us along the way, sometimes for a long time, sometimes for shorter seasons. During our ongoing search for direction, I had been doing prayer walks in the early morning hours before anyone was out of bed. A couple of dear brothers in the Lord, Ben and Josh, encouraged me to do it with them. We would do a three-way phone call, all walking near our own homes, where we would catch up with each other briefly and pray out loud as we walked. It was a refreshing learning time for me, something that really stretched me.

During many of those times, while we would be praying about something, God would draw my attention to something on my walk that would relate to what someone else was saying, and I would verbally turn that scene into a word picture as I continued the prayer. While I first thought they were isolated incidents, my brothers in Christ encouraged me that I had a gifting for translating something I saw into something relevant for someone else. It was a confirmation for me that I could take life moments and turn them into life lessons in real time.

Days and weeks passed. I had not forgotten about the little bridge on my shelf and had increased my interest in looking at rocks at the creek on our walks. On July 6, Katrina and I set out for another one of our adventures to our favorite place at the creek. I was on vacation from work that week, and we had been through a lot of busyness at home lately, so we needed a break, one of those days where we were in no hurry.

After our trip that day, I wrote the following story:

July 2020:

On this beautiful July morning I was blessed with some time off and enjoyed a leisurely bike ride with my lovely wife, Katrina. My sights were set on our spot down the road at the creek, which would give us a quiet opportunity to visit and pray together for the day. As the cool breeze blew in our faces down the highway, we were free to roam the countryside and enjoy the pleasant morning. We were off!

Arriving at the creek, I took the lead, parked my bike, and waited for her to come along. We sauntered down the short trail to the water and arrived to see the beauty of it all: water flowing past us, rippling water over rocks, and lazy schools of small fish without a care in the world. We quickly made our way across the large, fallen tree that had been our pathway across the creek for quite a while. As we hopped down from the tree trunk on the opposite side, we savored the cooler temperatures under the canopy of the trees. Although the July sun was beating down on us when we entered the forest, we were now in a cool, hidden wonderland. We walked down to the place we often went, a short hop back across the water to the beautiful river birch tree that towers over the creek bed. But when we came to the tree, Katrina didn't slow down.

"Look!" she said. "Someone must have built a bridge here!" I wasn't seeing it, but what I did see was a few random rocks in the middle of a somewhat treacherous area. A bridge it was not. I was the first to point out that the "bridge" she spoke of needed some serious construction before a crossing to uncharted territory could be attempted. So, she quickly gathered two or three additional rocks, added them to the "bridge," and proceeded to cross to the other side, rocks moving and tumbling as each footstep launched her across.

"Come on, baby!" she yelled as she headed down the creek like a whitetail deer headed into the wilderness, happy to be exploring new lands. I stayed behind.

As I watched her wander down the creek, I grew determined to make this pathway passable. With lots of wonderful building materials available, I wandered around identifying the most stable, bridge-worthy rocks that could be had. After no small effort, I managed to make a little one-lane route that allowed me to nimbly pass to the other side. But I wasn't satisfied in the least. Knowing we would have to pass back that way and having an abundance of new rocks handy on the opposite shore, I took ample time to neatly stack another row of rocks among the others, making a much more stable passageway for our return.

Off down the creek I wandered, seeking my beautiful bride, confident that we had safe passage for the return trip. I spotted her skipping and wandering upstream, happy as she could be. As I grew closer to her, I could see she had also crossed a pool of water using a pitiful-looking fallen tree that was frighteningly narrow at one end. Happy she was just across the pool and headed back, I watched her navigate the skinny balance beam and gingerly cross back to my side. We then strolled back down the creek the way we had come and sat down near the magnificent bridge I had built. After admiring my work, we sat, skipped a few rocks, talked, and prayed together. We sincerely asked God for clarity, peace, and direction for my work and our future. After our prayer time, we stood up, walked across my reinforced rock bridge, and made our way down the creek to retrieve our bikes and head back to the farm.

God revealed something amazing about my work situation as I unpacked the events of that day together. My sweet wife is as adventurous as can be, only glancing at minor risks and obstacles before plowing forward. I, on the other hand, am always the skeptic, the gatherer of all the facts. Not only do I want every bridge to be stable enough to cross, but I want it strong enough to handle a return trip. This was our work journey at that very moment: testing the waters, planning, building the bridge, and preparing to cross.

God had been using our time together in His beautiful creation to let the rocks cry out to us, to give us clear guidance. He was moving in ways we could not even imagine. From that day forward, I had peace about leaving my work. The time was nearing, and we knew it. Could the waters of the creek rise again one day and wash away that magnificent little foot bridge? Most likely. But we knew we had to cross to the opposite shore to discover what God had in store for us, putting our trust in Him. We just needed to wait a bit longer, until the time came for God to give us a bright, vivid green light. In the meantime, we could trust in God's promise:

> *For I know the thoughts that I think*
> *toward you, says the Lord,*
> *thoughts of peace and not of evil, to give*
> *you a future and a hope.*
> *Then you will call upon Me and go and*
> *pray to Me, and I will listen to you.*
> *And you will seek Me and find Me,*
> *when you search for Me with all your heart.*
> Jeremiah 29:11-13

18

Clarity

The late summer of 2020 was bearing down on us. The world was in shambles, and people were not sure what to do about much of anything. An important presidential election was looming over us, only months away. It was a time of confusion and major uncertainty for most.

During that time, after that peace had settled over me about my work, one word kept coming into my view from various, unexplainable places: "clarity." I had prayed at the creek that God would give me absolute clarity to know when to move on. Over the course of the next couple of months, after I prayed that prayer, I began to get random pieces of mail from ministries we had supported in the past that had the theme of clarity written all over them. I heard random messages from individuals about clarity. All I was hearing was the word clarity, clarity, clarity. Naturally, I interpreted it to mean I should wait until I had clarity, and that when it came from the Lord, I would know it without any doubts whatsoever.

Fall brought new rumblings of a storm that had begun brewing at work. A change was in the air, particularly in our department. As our manager began to plan for the remainder of the year and beyond, talks of a departmental restructure emerged. At that point, I had been in our marketing department for the better part of a dozen years, so news of that magnitude didn't shock or phase me in the least. I had seen it time and again. New titles, new focus, new this and new that. It was old hat to me, or so it seemed. In addition to the restructure talks, murmurings were beginning to surface about bringing everyone back into the office instead of working remotely. Some were elated about getting to go back into the office, having become sick of being cooped up at home, but I was not among that ecstatic group. Aside from all the work rumblings, God had been putting some pieces of the puzzle together for me personally, including some firm nudges that said, "I am going to do a work in you beyond what you are doing in this job. *You were created for something more.*"

As we were all on the edge of our seats at work waiting for the departmental changes to take place, we had a project of our own taking shape on the farm. It appeared when the previous owners of our property had completed construction on the house, they began the construction of a separate garage. However, the garage never progressed beyond a concrete pad. We had been parking there for a few years by that point, but God had blessed us with the finances to have a garage erected, which would provide some much-needed space. We were thinking of our short-term needs, but we were also considering the future and what God would have us to do as a family business. After no small effort getting all the arrangements made with a metal-building company, we were able to have the garage installed by the end of September.

In the summer and fall of that year, the financial blessings of having no mortgage or debt created surplus income, which allowed us to make some other improvements to our home. In addition to building the new garage, we replaced our aging heat and air unit, which had conveniently died in October, when it was neither hot nor cold. We were also "blessed" with a hailstorm, which gave us a new roof from the insurance company to replace the original fifteen-year-old roof. Being equipped with a new garage, new air unit, new roof, and a paid-for house gave us great peace of mind and thankfulness to God for providing. God really seemed to be putting our ducks in a row.

Before I could depart from my employer, I had a substantial list of things I wanted to have in place in our personal life, things that were important to me to have secured before we could move forward. The list was long, but I had been checking things off one by one. This was part of my process of planning my life the way I wanted it. That is why everyone wants to win the lottery, gain an inheritance, build their "castle," or heap up enough wealth, right? We think if we check enough things off the list and build enough safety and security into our lives, we will eliminate all the obstacles or hurdles that may come our way.

But the thing God kept bringing me back to, time and again, was that when God said it was time to go, we would go, regardless of the status of the list.

God's Word constantly reminds us of this :

But seek first the kingdom of God and His righteousness,
and all these things shall be added to you.
Matthew 6:33

Trust in the Lord with all your heart,
and lean not on your own understanding.
In all your ways acknowledge Him,
and He shall direct your paths.
Proverbs 3:5-6

Your word is a lamp unto my feet and a light unto my path.
Psalm 119:105

You know what all these verses say to me? They say if I seek God's Kingdom first and trust in Him with all that I am, He will make my paths straight, light them well, and meet my needs.

Another area of our lives Katrina and I were homing in on as we prayed about our future was that of limiting beliefs, or mindset. While it has been quite a journey (and still is), we began forming new habits of how we thought and talked. For example, in the years and months leading up to that time in our lives, I would continually say to myself, *If I leave my job, we are all going to be poor and starve to death.* Having now lived for a significant period since my employment ended, and considering my waistline, I can attest to you for certain that I have not dwindled to starvation. In fact, I am far from it. But well beyond that is the fact that looking back on my entire life, I can see God has always taken care of us. He always will.

The end of November brought our usual Thanksgiving celebrations with family. At work, we had been told a departmental meeting would be held upon our return from the holiday on Monday, the first day of December. It was a strange time because many of us hadn't seen much of each other in person, given the fact we had been working from home. The meeting was also a bit mysterious, because only certain individuals had been invited.

The Meeting

As we entered the building that first day of December and made our way to the giant auditorium for our Monday meeting, we were all instructed to sit far apart, masks on. It seemed odd that only a small number from our department were there, but we figured out quickly that those attending were essentially the managers of the department. It was also a dead giveaway that something was amiss, given that the human resources manager was also present.

The meeting began as our manager rolled out the final plans for our department restructure that had been talked about for months at that point. However, not long into the presentation, we were also told our current positions were being eliminated and we would be unemployed in two months.

Rumblings began in the room, and at that time our manager and the human resources manager went over our options, including the new positions we could all apply for. If we did nothing, our employment would cease in two months.

It was one of those slow-motion moments like you see in the movies, where you glance around the room and can't really hear anything that's being said as the sounds become muffled. Things became somewhat blurry as numbness settled around me; a feeling of warmth came over me as I took it all in. Not long into the conversations, while all the questions and answers began flying back and forth across the room, calmness and excitement simultaneously flooded through me.

"This is it," I said to myself. "This is the wide-open door out of here, the moment we've been praying for!"

Others were asking questions about the new jobs and how to apply. I tried to discreetly ask questions about the severance package and hide my smile. I was just ready for the meeting to be over so I could share the news with Katrina.

Things happened fast after that. I had two weeks to write a resume and apply for a job I didn't even want. I have to say, there were some brief moments of trepidation on my part as we pondered our options. Others were staying up late freshening up or creating their resumes. I was reading documentation to ensure I was doing everything right to receive my severance package. After confirmation with my wife, church family, and friends, we knew this was the moment we had been praying for, that God had put it in my lap and blessed us over and above anything we could ask for. He had given us a way out with crystal clarity. I would not be applying for a new position. It was time to go. This was the green light.

The next two months were a bit sketchy as far as work was concerned. While everyone else in the office was absorbed in the process of applying for jobs and securing their seats at the table, I was hiding in the shadows, biding my time, and preparing for my departure. It was easy. Years earlier, because I sensed I would not be staying indefinitely, I had turned my office at work into a minimalist workspace. Aside from a picture or two on my desk, I had essentially cleaned out everything that belonged to me.

One thing that did change for the worse those last two months, though, was my work schedule. It reverted to what it had been prior to us being sent home—three days at home, two days in the office. But it would be temporary, especially given that the Christmas holidays were arriving soon and I would only be working for the month of January thereafter. I was a bit sad knowing I had saved up several weeks of vacation to use during the holidays, and I wished I could just be away from the turmoil. But when I learned leftover vacation days would be paid to me in cash in my severance package, I figured I could wait another month and I would be on an indefinite vacation.

Christmas came and went, and then the new year arrived. With one month of employment left, I started assisting those who would be taking over my responsibilities, answering all their questions about the projects I had been working on. I also worked closely with our human resources department to ensure everything would be in place for my smooth departure. The bridge had been built, the rocks made steady, and we were about to cross. One month to go!

19

Crossing the Bridge

I need a holiday, a very long holiday,
and I don't expect I shall return.
In fact, I mean not to.
Bilbo Baggins[1]

There were many times in the years leading up to my departure from work when I envisioned leaving that place and moving on to other adventures life could bring our way. I remember many a time when I would drive to work, pull into the parking lot, and visually scan the parking lot and buildings, taking it all in as if I were about to say goodbye. Other times, I would come through the front door and pass all the cubicles and familiar faces, wondering when I would take that walk

---

1   The character of Bilbo Baggins, as quoted in the movie *The Lord of the Rings: The Fellowship of the Ring*, based on the book by the same name, by J.R.R. Tolkien.

for the last time. In most instances, those are the feelings people have as they approach their retirement years, not when they are fifty. But for me, that time indeed arrived early.

We experienced the hand of God in it all, likely in ways we will never know. He was working behind the scenes to put the pieces in place and to get us on the same page with Him so we could follow through with the transition. Some of His workings were obvious, such as the timing of it all and other details that fell into place. But God put the icing on the cake with His additional reassuring nods of approval.

God's confirmations are all around each of us. He provides them through people, circumstances, actions, objects, and opportunities—His ways are endless. When you are walking with God and close to His desires, your senses are wide open and He can show you things you wouldn't normally see, things most people would overlook in their everyday lives. It is awesome that He will not only take the time to show you the way, but He will also give you little nudges forward. God loves to walk alongside us, put His arm over our shoulder, and say, "Yes, you are headed in the right direction. This is the way."

After working most of 2020 from home, the return to two days per week in the office felt strange. On one of those first days back, after sitting in my chair for the better part of the day looking at the same four walls, I asked myself how in the world I had done this for so long. How had I found pleasure in that small square of existence, day in and day out, for years?

I decided to stand up for a minute to give my legs a stretch and enjoy the sun out the window on that cool December day. I walked over to the window, raised the blinds, and observed the cars driving by on the busy street. Then the oddest thing happened. I looked over to the left of the window, and just outside, in the brown winter grass, stood a small construction sign that read, "Danger, Confined Space." I chuckled to myself, thinking how God's comedic timing was perfect. He knew I needed another confirmation I was headed in the right direction. Yes, that little sign had been placed there by some construction worker who had been doing work in a hole down below the street. But little did that guy know that God had guided his hand in putting that sign there for me as well, to shout out to me as boldly as a flashing neon sign.

Yes, I had been in the confined space of that office for more than my fair share. I had entered that office a dozen years earlier, excited and ambitious to be there. I would now be leaving through the same door, perhaps with the same smile on my face and spirit in my step. I had been right where I needed to when I made myself at home in that office, walking in the direction God had for us. Although I would now be going in the opposite direction through that door, it was an amazing feeling to know I would still be moving in God's direction.

The bridge had been built, and a very solid one at that. God's hands had been constructing it, and it was nearing the time for us to cross. I would not be leaving empty-handed but with full pay for the better part of the year ahead, along with other benefits that came with my severance package. I had done well in maintaining good standing with my employer, which left the door wide open for me to return in the future should the opportunity arise. My boss had even accepted my request to spend my last month of employment working from home. This is the value of keeping your bridges intact and never burning them. You never know when your journey may require you to pass that way once again: "If it is possible, as much as it depends on you, live peaceably with all men" (Romans 12:18).

Nearing the end of my corporate career in January 2021 was surreal, almost like waiting for Christmas or a grand birthday celebration. Were we almost there, near the finish line? We were stable financially, but by no means in any position to officially retire. Although some may think we accumulated an amazingly massive financial storehouse after twenty-eight years of employment, we just weren't there. Did we have some savings? Yes. Was it unlimited? Not in the least. Life had happened, which brought many setbacks along the way. In the years before our wonderful marriage, before we met, Katrina and I had both survived the shipwreck of divorce. We are both acquainted with the word "hard." We have been blessed with an amazing marriage and family, which have required diligent work and financial discernment from day one but have reaped a bounty of blessings that has yet to be contained. We now reached a new precipice, a moment we had been praying for, waiting for. It was an opportunity to step out into the unknown again. We had lots of unanswered questions, and we still do.

The last week of my employment mostly entailed cleaning up my work and handing it off to others, getting them ready to take over where I would leave off. Things were slowing down for me there, and I had already taken the time to pack anything lingering in my office. On my last day of work, I attended a very nice luncheon my boss had arranged for some of our closest colleagues. We enjoyed a wonderful meal together, visiting with one another and telling stories of times past. They were all very kind and blessed me with a nice gift for my early retirement. It was bittersweet. I had spent the last twenty-eight years in that place, most of my adult life. I had created friends and memories to last a lifetime. It was a very nice departure, indeed.

Earlier in the week, prior to my last day at work, God had blessed us with an unseasonably warm day on Monday of that week, so naturally, Katrina and I took a walk to Shiloh Creek after lunch. Like two newlyweds out for a date, we strolled a mile down the road to that familiar oak. We ducked into the brush, down the hill, past the beaver camp, and over to our beloved river birch along the water's edge. Signs of fall still lingered as leaves collected near the makeshift bridge I had made many months earlier. I took a few minutes to straighten some rocks and make them stable, pleased that the water had not overrun the bridge and messed it up too much. We crossed over to the other side and downstream, happy to be wandering a bit on that warm day.

As we walked and talked among the thousands of random rocks, we made our way to the long pool of water south of the bridge crossing. It looked like as good a place as any to stop, take a seat on the rocks, and lift our voices to God in prayer. Katrina and I both prayed as we enjoyed the quiet trickle of the water flowing nearby. We had visited this spot many times now in our journeys. After our prayer time, I sat amid the endless floor of loose rocks, gazing at the complexity and variety of them all, knowing God had put every one of them there, molding them and shaping them over the course of time. Then suddenly, one caught my eye.

I reached down to pick up the rock, rolled it around in my hand, and noticed its unique shape. Brushing some dirt off, it became clear to me. In the palm of my hand, I was holding a perfectly crafted capital "A." That small piece of sandstone had not been crafted by any mere mortal, but by the Master Craftsman Himself. I pondered what the meaning of the rock could be. Nothing immediately came to mind.

After our wonderful time with the Lord and the discovery of my latest treasure, we walked up the creek, sauntered across the rock bridge, passed the beaver camp, scrambled up the hill, and returned to the oak tree. Taking each other by the hand, we headed back to the farm.

Imagine yourself on a hike. You study the map at the trailhead, get a good idea of your destination, and then take off down the trail for an adventure in the woods. You pass by a lake, enjoy the variety of wildflowers, scale an enormous outcropping of rocks, and follow the trail upward to an amazing scenic overlook that displays God's beauty in all its splendor. While the path seems well-used and clear for the most part, at times it becomes hard to discern, and you wonder if you've strayed from the trail. Then as you begin to doubt your steps, you come upon a very clear marker at eye level, firmly affixed to a strong tree. That marker gives you confidence to carry on, move ahead with boldness, and continue your hike through the woods. As you hike on, you are grateful someone came before you to not only blaze the trail but mark it clearly.

Arriving back home, as I contemplated the stone I held in my hand, it finally came to me. It was like when you see a familiar face at the store you've not seen in years. You rack your brain trying to think of their name, and then it comes to you, as if you have switched on a light. I had to do a little digging in one of my old journals from a few years back, but I finally found it. There it was: the letter "A."

I held the rock up to a sketch I had made four years prior. There, in my notebook journal, was the identical letter "A," pretty much the same size and shape. I had crafted that letter as part of the logo for Almost Home Farm. Is it any wonder the Architect of the world could give me an idea four years prior, one that matched up exactly with the piece of stone I was holding in my hand? It doesn't surprise me in the least, and yet I was absolutely blown away at God for taking the time to remind me He was with us and aware of our needs, guiding our steps and our direction. It wasn't like I had found a rock and *then* created a logo: it was the exact reverse. God put it in my heart to create what He wanted, and then four years later, He sent me a confirmation that we were headed in the right direction.

So, where is that direction? Well, we are sojourners traveling toward our ultimate destination, our home beyond the skies. Our temporary dwelling place, our farm, is more than an earthly destination. Almost Home is the idea that we are not to plant our feet too firmly to this earth, a home, or any destination on this planet. Yes, four years before this walk in the woods, during this *exact same week* in 2017, God had impressed upon me the idea of our farmhouse only being temporary. We needed to look heavenward to our destination, our final home. This didn't mean we would settle for the farmhouse and then start looking for another one when we tired of it. It meant we would settle into our home until God took us home or elsewhere Himself.

God used that rock that day as a spiritual marker for us. He walked alongside us, put a rock in front of me, and said, "I know this is a hard transition for you, but you're headed down the right path. Continue, stay the course."

The Maker of the universe and our world, who stopped to whisper in my ear four years earlier and gave me the vision for Almost Home Farm, has dropped many spiritual clues along our path. Was it just a rock the shape of a bridge or one shaped like the letter "A" that moved us in a new direction? Oh, no. Those were just the icing on the cake, God's dessert at the bountiful feast of His endless blessings.

Yes, God still speaks. Are you listening?

Epilogue
Afterthoughts

Yesteryear is in the history books; yesterday is gone forever. We can never get them back. But the good news is those years of our lives that brought us to the place we are now were foundational. Sometimes, that foundation has been well-built and able to withstand the test of time and the onslaught of storms. Other foundations need to be ripped up, re-established, leveled to the ground, rebuilt, restabilized.

The culmination of everything in this book has been a lifelong work, to say the least. In years past, when I thought I was ready to write my story, I had to pause, wait, and clear away the clutter in my mind and heart to prepare for what God was doing in me through this work. This book and its words have been fervently prayed over as I sought the Lord for His words and not mine. Throughout the writing process, I consistently prayed and reminded God I was committing this work to Him, as Scripture teaches us:

Commit your works to the Lord,
And your thoughts will be established.
Proverbs 16:3

In this book, I have presented a few ways God moved in our lives to challenge us and give us clear direction. God still moves in miraculous ways today. He is still the same God who made the earth from nothing, speaking it into existence. He still commands the winds and the waves, and they obey.

Try as we might, we cannot contain or recreate a "God moment." That is His business and His alone. In life, we occasionally see something amazing happen, knowing God put that instance right in front of us. Then we spend a lot of our own energy trying to recreate that moment, as if it had anything to do with us in the first place—believe me, I am one of the world's worst at trying this. It is God who moves. Our job is to make ourselves available to Him, to remove the distractions of life, to lean in, and to listen with our entire being.

God works through a flash of lightning, in the voice of a child, through a random act of kindness at the grocery store, or with an unexpected gift from a friend. Perhaps the police officer giving you a ticket for your transgression has slowed you down for a moment to save your life from a head-on collision just up ahead. Yes, God is there every step of the way, bringing wonderful changes to your life. Sometimes it happens when you least expect it, and other times it happens as you're looking and waiting with eyes wide open. Live expectantly. Your heavenly Father is crazy about you and wants to give you, His child, good gifts, often and generously. That's the kind of God we serve.

Please know we do not take the statements in this book lightly, as if we were guided by a stone or treated chance encounters as gospel truth. Everything God guides us through in our daily walk must be measured against God's holy Scriptures, the Holy Spirit, and the Holy Spirit working in God's people who come alongside us. As we listen to family, coworkers, neighbors, circumstances, dreams, visions, or whatever unique way God chooses to speak, He will never reveal anything that is contrary to Scripture, His ways, or His nature.

My prayer is that I am found faithful to God's calling on my life, wherever that leads me. As I pursue my talents and giftings, may I never settle for anything less than walking along holding God's hand as He leads the way. May I never be consumed by a house on the hill, a car in the driveway, or the treasure in my bank account. May I walk each day trusting in God's faithful provisions, which He has promised to those who are His. All the blessings and possessions that have been given to me in this life— and they are many—have come from God the Father, and it all belongs to Him. May I be found pursuing God's desires with all my heart, soul, mind, and strength.

I know for certain God is preparing a place for me for when I reach His glorious Kingdom. Until that time, although the farmhouse seems to be all we need now, I still have a bit of an itch that may need scratching at some point. Perhaps there is yet another bridge to cross or another place to pursue in this world. I sure hate moving, but you never know!

I can't help but dream of another home, if God were to move us again in this life. Picture this: At the edge of a quiet country road, a gravel driveway disappears into a vast expanse of woods, slightly turning to the right and out of sight, under the shadow of a canopy of trees. Rumor has it a little cottage sits at the far end of that quaint drive, which takes you across an old rock bridge from yesteryear. Crossing the bridge, you take in the breathtaking expanse of the creek in either direction as the magnificent waters flow beneath. Upon your arrival, a sweet little couple greets you from their swing on the front porch. They are happy you have arrived as you embrace their hospitality and settle into their otherworldliness.

It will feel like you are Almost Home.

About the Author

A typical farm boy from the South, David Steen grew up in pursuit of the American Dream. After college graduation, he staked his claim in the corporate world as an accomplished Senior Designer in Engineering, followed by an adventurous career as a Product Manager. His calling and passion to write, incubating for decades, manifested itself through personal and professional blogging, as well as a plethora of published articles for various magazines.

David resides on a small farm in Hartford, Arkansas, where he enjoys long walks to the creek with his lovely wife and short walks through the field with his sheep. Other passions include writing, music, reading, cooking for their large family, and sipping on a cup of dark roast coffee as often as possible.

www.almosthomebooks.com

A free ebook edition is available with the purchase of this book.

To claim your free ebook edition:

1. Visit MorganJamesBOGO.com
2. Sign your name CLEARLY in the space
3. Complete the form and submit a photo of the entire copyright page
4. You or your friend can download the ebook to your preferred device

Morgan James BOGO™

A **FREE** ebook edition is available for you or a friend with the purchase of this print book.

CLEARLY SIGN YOUR NAME ABOVE

Instructions to claim your free ebook edition:
1. Visit MorganJamesBOGO.com
2. Sign your name CLEARLY in the space above
3. Complete the form and submit a photo of this entire page
4. You or your friend can download the ebook to your preferred device

Print & Digital Together Forever.

Snap a photo

Free ebook

Read anywhere

Printed in the USA
CPSIA information can be obtained
at www.ICGtesting.com
JSHW022306010923
47738JS00005B/7